# ORIENTAL RUG REPAIR

## by Peter F. Stone

1981
Chicago, Illinois

First edition

Library of Congress
Catalog Card No.: 81-82388

Stone, Peter F.
    Oriental Rug Repair

ISBN 0-940582-00-7

Published by
Greenleaf Company
P.O. Box 11393
Chicago, Illinois 60611

# ACKNOWLEDGEMENTS

A primary resource for this book has been the wide experience and thorough knowledge of Maury Bynum. He has shared these as consultant and reviewer in the preparation of this work. Maury's skill in rug repair and high standards of craftsmanship have served as a model to me and to his able assistants.

I am grateful to Chris Rolik for her helpful criticism, knowledgeable suggestions and photographs of repairs in process. The excellent repair results achieved by Chris Rolik are equally due to her patient care and highly developed technique.

Bob Luckey is responsible for the typography and design of this book. He has been generous with sound advice on graphics, layout and book production.

Betty Dayron has my affectionate gratitude for her encouragement and her patience with my frustrations and enthusiasms during this project.

PFS

# Oriental Rug Repair

# Contents

# Introduction

In the last ten years, there's been an almost explosive demand for oriental rugs. Many of these rugs have moved off the floor and on to the wall to be appreciated as works of art. Appreciation has been monetary as well as aesthetic. Current prices of oriental rugs reflect their rarity and new status. And as the prices rise, basements and attics are rummaged for that old oriental rug once thought to be incompatible with modern decor.

Because of their increasing value, oriental rugs that were destined for the scrap heap are now repaired and restored. Owners of contemporary oriental rugs preserve their investments by having damage repaired promptly. The demand for rug repair services has never been greater. Yet, very few people know how to repair oriental rugs.

Rug repairs are not as difficult as many suppose. There's nothing difficult about a Turkish knot or a Persian knot. Tying them is easier than tying a shoelace. Anyone who can develop needlecraft skills can acquire the skills used in oriental rug repair. The primary requisites are attention to detail and patience.

Knowledge of oriental rug repair techniques can be helpful even to those who don't intend to apply those techniques. Dealers and collectors can use this information to evaluate the repairability and price of worn or damaged rugs on the market. Perhaps the greatest reward in repairing oriental rugs is the knowledge that one is preserving something beautiful. And that the effort of repair and restoration benefits everyone who will find pleasure in viewing the rug.

For our purposes, an oriental rug is a hand-knotted rug with pile knots tied using the symmetric (Turkish) or asymmetric (Persian) knot. Many of these rugs have flatwoven or killim ends. The repair techniques described for killim ends are generally appropriate for flatwoven rugs.

# Chapter 1

# Whether to Repair

It may seem strange to begin a book on repairing oriental rugs by questioning the desirability of repair. But the beginning is the best point because this is the question you must ask yourself before *you* begin any repair. In this chapter, we'll look at the factors that can affect your decision. Among these factors are the alternatives to repair: restoration and conservation. Depending on the circumstances, either one may be preferable to repair.

## Restoration

Restoration is an attempt to return an object to its original or first condition. The erosions of wear, chance and time are removed by re-creating portions of the object. A true restoration of a rug requires the same type of animal and vegetable fibers in the same types of yarn colored with the same types of dyes as the original rug. And the construction features of the restoration must be the same as the original. This may seem overly elaborate, but some rugs merit this treatment. Most restorations are a compromise; some details of the original are not reproduced.

One approach to restoration is to cannibalize a rug of the same type, origin and age. In fact, this was done in the restoration of the greatest example of classical rugmaking, the Ardabil carpet.[1] Originally, there were two of these 16th century Persian carpets, a matched pair. The Ardabil carpet in the Victoria and Albert Museum was restored in about 1890 by using large parts of its pair, now in the Los Angeles County Museum of Art.

True restoration is more expensive than either conservation or repair. When is this expense justified? The answer depends on the rarity and value of the rug. Rarity and value are very different qualities. For example, a rug that is an artifact of a disappearing tribal culture might be rare without being monetarily valuable. A rug may be monetarily valuable without being rare, such as a factory-made finely knotted silk rug. And some rugs are both valuable *and* rare. As a rule the expense of true restoration is not justified unless the rug is extremely valuable. Otherwise, the investment in restoration is lost. If a rug is extremely valuable *and* rare, then its rarity is likely to justify conservation by an expert.

## Conservation

Conservation is preserving an object with as little change to the object as possible. The goal is to prevent further damage or deterioration. Continuing deterioration may be due to chemical changes, insect or microbial attack, exposure to heat, light, moisture or the atmosphere. Deterioration may result from the way an item is displayed. For instance, a rug can be structurally damaged when one edge is used to hang the whole rug or a rug may be faded through continued exposure to direct sunlight. Conservation does not necessarily sequester an object in a time capsule or the museum attic. However, methods of mounting, display or storage do prevent further wear or damage.

Here are a few principles[2] that govern textile conservation:

- Treatment must not damage the original fabric and the loss of original material must be minimized.

- Chemicals used for cleaning, to kill insects or fungus, or for other treatment of the fabric must be completely removable.

- The minimum amount of chemical to produce the desired result should be used.

- Mechanical methods of preservation, if sufficient, are preferable to chemical treatment.

- As much as possible, conservation techniques must preserve the original pliability texture, sheen, and color of the fabric.

There is a type of textile damage that cannot be halted by conservation procedures. This type of damage is described by conservators as "inherent vice" (not to be confused with original sin). Inherent vice causes a fabric, or any work of art to self-destruct because of the materials used or the method of construction. The gradual disintegration of rug pile with the passage of time when certain dyes have been used is an example of inherent vice.

Presumably, items to be conserved are rare and have exceptional scientific, historic, or artistic value. The item is conserved because:

- with further study it will yield additional information, or

- it is historically significant and part of the human heritage of one generation to its successor, or

- it is beautiful and should be preserved for the enjoyment of others.

Some items, including certain oriental rugs, should be conserved for all of these reasons.

Are you or I likely to come across rugs so rare that they should be conserved rather than restored or repaired? It's possible. That possibility should encourage you to learn as much as you can about oriental rugs. The knowledge will prevent you from repairing that priceless Mamluk.

## Repair

Repair is a compromise between the poles of conservation and true restoration. Repair conserves rugs because it minimizes further deterioration through normal use or handling. Repair is restoration to the extent it truly copies the original materials and construction of a rug.

The purpose of a repair influences the kind of work to be done on a rug. For example, the repair of a torn selvage may differ in technique and materials depending on whether the purpose of the repair is to:

1. stabilize the rug structure to prevent further damage

2. prepare the rug for continued use

3. re-create the artistic merit of the rug

Although it's generally desirable to make unobtrusive repairs, this is most important if the purpose of the repair is to re-create the artistic merit of the piece. In this case, repair is closer to restoration and accordingly more difficult and expensive.

## Does it pay to repair?

To decide whether repair makes sense in dollars and cents, there are three things you must know or estimate.

1. The market value of the damaged rug

2. The cost of repairs

3. The market value of the repaired rug

In the rug market, one plus two does *not* equal three. We'll take a closer look at these quantities before we try to add them up.

The *market value of the damaged rug* is based on an estimate of the value of an undamaged rug of the same type, size, age and general condition minus the loss in value due to the damage. Your sources for rug valuation are either personal familiarity with the rug market or appraisal. Familiarity with the rug market is developed slowly by tracking rug prices in stores, galleries and auctions. If you suspect a rug needing repair may be of exceptional value, then the cost of an expert opinion or appraisal is worthwhile.

The *cost of repair* depends on the skill and time needed for the repair. Since you're doing the repair work yourself, you have an advantage over someone who is out-of-

pocket for the cost of repairs. But how much time and skill *are* required?

As an overall guide to the difficulty of repairs, here are major repairs in order from least to greatest difficulty:

1. Reknotting worn areas

2. Reconstructing warp and weft to repair holes

3. Reconstructing selvage and adjacent areas

4. Reconstructing rug ends and adjacent areas

This is the order in which these repairs will be explained in the text.

Your own experience is the best guide to the time, skill and effort needed for a particular repair. However, the relative difficulty of repairs and approximate time requirements will be discussed in the chapters dealing with specific repairs.

The *market value of the repaired rug* is surprisingly variable. At the low end, the post-repair market value can be *lower* than the market value of the original damaged rug. At the high end, the post-repair market value can be a great deal more than the sum of the value of the damaged rug and the cost of repairs.

A repaired rug can be worth less than the same rug in a damaged state if the rug should have been conserved rather than repaired. In repair, damaged material is removed. For an extremely rare rug, the removal of *any* material lowers its value. There are some rugs that cannot be repaired and the attempt produces further damage. This can happen when the foundation of a rug has rotted or is fragile or embrittled with age. Repairs can lower the value of a rug if they are not skillfully done or are not consistent in quality with the rug as a whole. Finally, costly repairs can produce a net loss when they are invested in a rug of poor quality in design or workmanship.

An oriental rug, like any object, can have a unique and personal value to its owner. The owner may well choose to pay the cost of repairs regardless of this investment's contribution to the rug's market value.

But repair of a rug can also be a very profitable investment. The relative value added to a rug by repairs is likely to be greatest under these conditions:

1. The damage is very obvious (in the center of the field, for example).

2. Repairs are skillfully done.

3. The cost of the repairs is low in comparison to the market value of the damaged rug.

Of course, it's possible to buy a rug that's greatly undervalued because of damage. This is a fine opportunity for someone who understands repair work and can correctly estimate the market value of the repaired rug. There are likely to be many of these opportunities as the prices of oriental rugs continue to rise.

### Skill level and repair—
### a cautionary word

One should not attempt repairs beyond one's skill level since poorly executed repairs lower the value of a rug. Rug repair is a craft requiring knowledge and skill. The knowledge is easier to acquire than the skill, a condition that leads to over-confidence. Bear in mind that, for the beginner, there is a very strong tendency to significantly *under* estimate the amount of time and work needed to perform a repair of acceptable quality.

Both experience and practice are needed to build skill. Beginning skill should be developed with worn and worthless rugs or scraps of rugs. Begin your practice with

coarsely woven rugs of less than fifty knots per square inch before working on more tightly knotted rugs. Practice on these until you are confident of your technique. Only then should you try a similar repair of a good or useable rug.

### Whether to repair
### is an investment decision

We've raised some points you should think about in deciding whether to repair a rug. Many of these points have been negative or counter indications to repair. It's simpler to describe these counter indications because almost all damage to oriental rugs *is* repairable. Practically, whether or not you repair a rug depends on the nature and extent of damage, for this determines the time and energy you must invest in the piece. A knowledge of rug structure is equally the basis for evaluating damage and making repairs. So, the subject of the next chapter will help you with your investment decision.

1. I. Bennett, *Rugs and Carpets of the World.* A and W Publications, 1977, p.45

2. S. E. Schur, *Technology and Conservation,* Spring, 1979, p.26

# Chapter 2

# Rug Structure and Technical Analysis

One must understand the construction of a rug before one can *re*construct it. The goal is to duplicate the structure and materials that were originally used for the rug under repair. The same materials, whether wool, cotton or silk. The same knot, whether symmetric or asymmetric and the same knot density. The same color, size and type of yarn wherever possible.

The diagrams in this chapter illustrate most of the terms used in "technical analysis." Technical analysis is identifying the materials and structural features of a specific rug. Technical analysis is the first step in any repair. You will find it easier to follow this discussion of technical analysis if you closely examine several oriental rugs as we discuss the structural features of oriental rugs.

Throughout this book, technical analyses accompany photographs of rugs wherever possible. By studying these analyses and photographs, you will develop your ability to identify structural features when you see them. By comparing these analyses, you will become familiar with the range and typical combinations of structural features.

The technical analyses are presented in this format:

*Provenance:* rug origin or common identification

*Pile:* type of fiber in pile yarn, type of knot, number of knots per square inch

*Warp:* type of fiber in warp yarn, warp ply, final direction of spin

*Weft:* type of fiber in weft yarn, number of wefts between rows of knots, weft ply, final direction of spin

All of these technical features are explained in this chapter.

## The rug weaving process

The foundation of a rug is a grid of warp and weft. This grid imposes a rectangular shape on the rug as a whole, as well as a rectilinearity on rug designs. Imagine drawing on a sheet of graph paper. You can draw whatever you like, as long as you draw on the existing lines. The result is that the size of the grid controls the fineness of detail in your drawing. So does the grid of warp and weft determine the fineness of detail in rug designs.

There are a variety of loom types used in the middle east. Some looms are vertical and the rug is wound on a roller beam as it is woven. For other vertical looms, the weaver sits on a plank that is raised as the rug is woven and the work level moves upwards on the loom frame. There are horizontal looms, generally nomadic, that consist of a frame or only stakes driven into the ground with crosspieces attached.

Regardless of the type of loom, the rug weaving process remains the same. Parallel yarns running the length of the loom, called "warps", are fixed to beams at either end of the loom. There are two sets of warps with alternating warps in different sets. If warps are numbered sequentially, then one set would be odd-numbered warps and the other set would be even-numbered warps. Suppose the set of odd-numbered warps is raised. This permits a shuttle carrying the weft yarn to pass horizontally between the two sets. This space between the two sets of warps where the shuttle passes is termed a "shed". Then the set of even-numbered warps is raised, permitting the shuttle to return through the shed and weave another

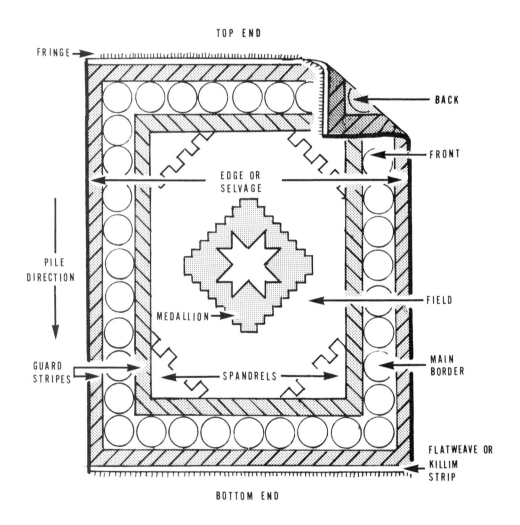

Figure 2-1. Basic design features of an oriental pile rug. Note, especially, the terms describing the rug orientation.

8

weft through the warps. A row of knots is tied on the warps and then more wefts are woven. There may be one or more wefts between each row of knots.

The rug, then, consists of wefts woven through the warps alternating with rows of knots tied to the warps. Warps are the most important structural element of the rug since they support both weft and knots. The combination of warp and weft is referred to as the "foundation".

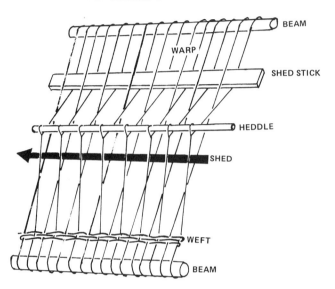

Figure 2-2. A simple loom showing the shed when the heddle is raised. Even-numbered warps (left to right) are raised.

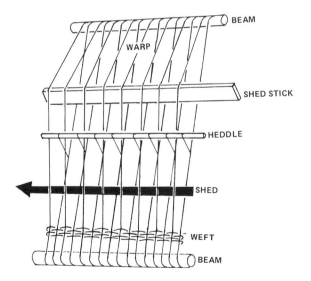

Figure 2-3. A simple loom showing the shed when the heddle is lowered. Odd-numbered warps (left to right) are raised due to the position of the shed stick.

## Warp and weft

On a loom, warps run the length of the loom. Wefts are horizontal yarn woven through the warps. Warp yarns may be made of cotton, wool or silk. Warp yarn is usually the heaviest yarn in a rug. Warps are usually undyed. Naturally colored wool is often used for warps.

Wefts are normally smaller in diameter than warps. They may be white, the natural colors of wool or dyed. Natural brown wool is often used for wefts in village and nomadic rugs. Wefts cannot be seen from the front of an unworn pile rug, so this is a way to use wool that cannot be dyed because of its natural color. The color of wefts can be characteristic for certain types of rugs. Blue wefts in Sarouks or red or pink wefts in Afshars, for example. A single weft woven through warps is termed a "shoot". The number of shoots between each row of knots is also characteristic for certain types of rugs. A single shoot between each row of knots is typical of Hamadans. Variation of two to eight shoots between rows of knots within the same rug is typical of Kazaks.

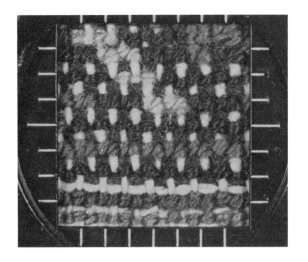

Figure 2-4. A rug back showing single wefts. Note that alternate warps can be seen (vertical yarn) crossing each weft.
*Provenance:* Hamadan mat
*Pile:* wool, symmetric knot, 64 knots per sq. in.
*Warp:* cotton, 5-ply, "S" spun overall
*Weft:* cotton, 1 shoot, 2-ply, "Z" spun overall

Figure 2-6. A rug back showing variation in weft count. There are two to five wefts between rows of knots.
*Provenance:* Anatolian yastik
*Pile:* wool, symmetric knot, 32 knots per sq. in.
*Warp:* wool, 2-ply, "S" spun overall
*Weft:* wool, 2-5 shoots, single, "Z" spun

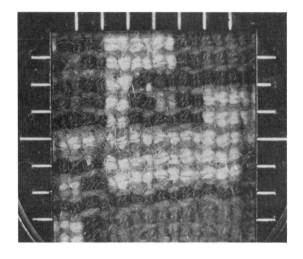

Figure 2-5. A rug back showing two wefts. Note that wefts are slightly staggered on adjacent warps and that all warps are concealed.
*Provenance:* Afshar, saddle bag face
*Pile:* wool, symmetric knot, 94 knots per sq. in.
*Warp:* wool, 2-ply, "S" spun overall
*Weft:* wool, 2 shoots, single, "Z" spun overall

## Warp offset

Usually warps are level and in the same plane within the rug. For some types of rugs, however, alternate warps are offset or depressed. This warp offset depends on the way warps are set up on the loom and differences in tension between wefts.

Suppose each row of knots is followed by two wefts. For each pair of wefts, the first weft is pulled quite taut and the return weft is woven loosely through the warps. The weft that is pulled taut, termed the "cable" weft, forces the warps into two planes. One plane will contain odd-numbered warps and the other plane will contain even-numbered warps. The second weft is loosely woven and termed the "sinuous" weft. The sinuous weft may be of lighter weight yarn than the cable weft.

This relationship between adjacent warps, each in different planes, can be described in degrees of rotation. For example, alternate warps can be offset 45 degrees or as much as 90 degrees. Where warps are offset about 45 degrees, the back of the rug has a characteristic ribbed appearance. Where warps are offset 90 degrees, one set of warps, odd-numbered for example, will lie on top of the set of even-numbered warps.

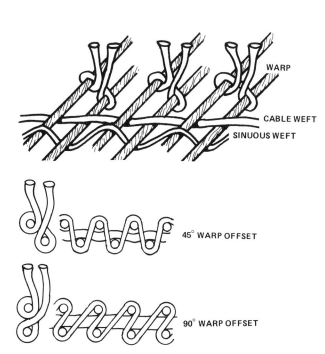

Figure 2-7. Warp offset with symmetric knot. Adjacent warps are in different planes, separated by the cable weft.

## Pile direction

Knots are tied in rows on the warps. The bottom of a rug is the end along which the first row of knots is tied. The two loose ends of each knot make up the pile of the rug. When the knots are tightened, the weaver pulls the ends downward. This give the pile a consistent direction. The tufts lie so the ends are towards the bottom of the rug. As each row of knots is tied, the pile covers the preceding row of knots like shingles on a roof.

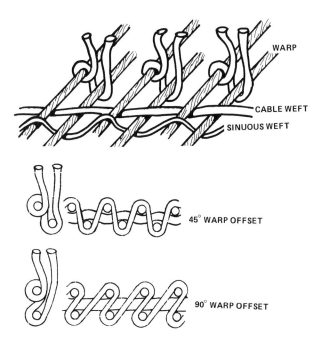

Figure 2-8. Warp offset with asymmetric knot. Adjacent warps are in different planes, separated by the cable weft.

The direction of the pile towards the bottom of the rug can be seen and felt. When one looks at a rug from the bottom towards the top, colors are darker than if one looks from the top towards the bottom. Light is absorbed by the pile ends, deepening colors when one looks from the bottom towards the top. Light is reflected from the sides of the pile, lightening colors when one looks from the top towards the bottom of a rug.

If one strokes the pile of a rug from the bottom towards the top, one can feel the resistance of the pile ends. This same resistance is not felt when one strokes from top to bottom.

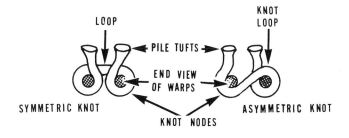

Figure 2-9. Descriptive terms for parts of the knot.

11

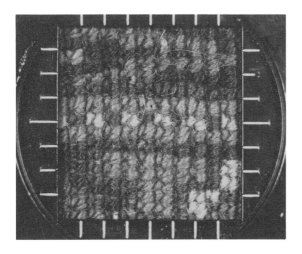

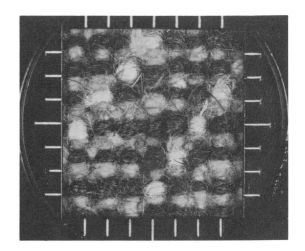

Figure 2-10. A warp offset of about 45°. The back of the rug has a ribbed appearance.
*Provenance:* Salor
*Pile:* wool, asymmetric knot open to the right, 165 knots per sq. in.
*Warp:* wool, 2-ply, "Z" spun overall
*Weft:* wool, 2 shoots, single, "Z" spun

Figure 2-12. A warp offset of about 90°. There is no ribbing; the back appears flat. Note that only one node is visible for each white knot.
*Provenance:* Fars (modern)
*Pile:* wool, asymmetric knot open to left, 56 knots per sq. in.
*Warp:* cotton, 2-ply, "Z" spun overall
*Weft:* cotton, 2 shoots, single, "Z" spun

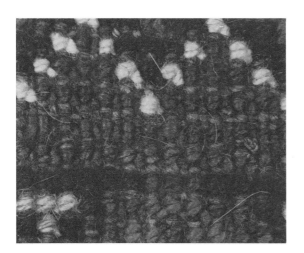

Figure 2-11. A warp offset of about 60°. The back of the rug has a ribbed appearance. Note the white knot nodes. One of the two knot nodes for each knot is barely visible. Compare these knot nodes to those shown in Figure 2-6 where there is no warp offset.
*Provenance:* Qashqai
*Pile:* wool, asymmetric knot open to left, 64 knots per sq. in.
*Warp:* wool, 2-ply, "S" spun overall
*Weft:* wool, 2 shoots, single "Z" spun overall

Figure 2-13. Cross-section of a tightly woven rug with a 45° warp offset. Note the back of the rug on which the cross-section is resting. Only one knot node is visible for each knot.
*Provenance:* Kashan
*Pile:* wool, asymmetric knot open to the left, 323 knots per sq. in.
*Warp:* cotton, 3-ply, "Z" spun overall
*Weft:* cotton, 2 shoots, 3-ply, "Z" spun overall

The design of a rug may indicate its top and bottom by the orientation of flowers or animals in the design. A prayer rug has a representation of a mihrab or prayer niche at the top. It usually appears as a stylized arch. These design indications of top and bottom are usually the same as indicated by the direction of the pile.

## Knots

The two basic knots used in oriental rugs are the symmetric, also called Turkish or Ghiordes and the asymmetric, also called Persian or Senneh. These knots are tied on two warps. If either of these knots are tied on four or more warps, it is termed a Jufti knot.

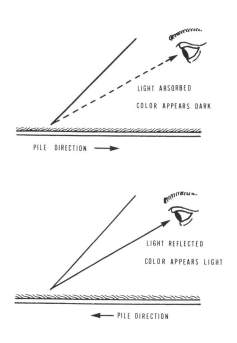

Figure 2-14. The effect of pile direction on apparent color.

It's difficult to identify the type of knot from the back of a rug. Close inspection of the front of the rug, especially worn areas, reveals the type of knot used. If there are no worn spots exposing the knot, pull the pile

up towards the top of the rug to expose the knot of the lower row. Choose an area where there are contrasting colors and be careful not to confuse weft or warp with the knot itself. A magnifying glass helps.

The symmetric knot always has a loop crossing two warps when viewed from the front of the rug. You can see both tufts emerging from underneath this loop.

If the loop crosses only one warp and only one tuft emerges from under the loop then the knot is asymmetric. The asymmetric knot can be open to the left or open to the right. This can be felt, as well as seen. With the asymmetric knot, the pile does not point directly to the bottom of the rug; it lies diagonally to the right or left depending on the way the asymmetric knot is tied. By stroking the rug, you can find the diagonal direction of greatest resistance. The asymmetric knot is open towards the side of the rug where the greatest resistance is felt.

A diagonal direction of the pile may also occur with the symmetric knot. If the weaver tightens a symmetric knot by pulling the ends sharply to the right or left and there is no warp offset, then the pile will lie diagonally.

Knots are tied on two warps. Where there is no warp offset, the knot loops around the two warps can be seen from the back of the rug. These two loops are termed "nodes". See Figure 2-9. There are two nodes whether the symmetric or asymmetric knot is used. That's why it's difficult to tell the knot type by looking at the *back* of the rug. When warps are highly offset, determining the type of knot can be very difficult even from the *front* of the rug.

For each knot, two nodes are visible from the back when there is no warp offset. From the back, then, there will be pairs of colored nodes. In general, if you can see only a *single* knot node of one color, this indicates warps in the rug are heavily offset. The other node of the pair is concealed because warps lie on top of each other.

Figure 2-15. Symmetric knots.

Figure 2-16. Symmetric knots. Note the tufts emerging from under the knot loops.
*Provenance:* Yoruk
*Pile:* wool, symmetric knot, 64 knots per sq. in.
*Warp:* wool, 2-ply, "Z" spun overall
*Weft:* wool, 3 shoots, single, "S" spun

Figure 2-17. Asymmetric knots open to the right.

Figure 2-18. Asymmetric knots open to the right. Note the tufts emerging to the right of the loops. No tufts pass under the loops.
*Provenance:* Tekke
*Pile:* wool, asymmetric knot open to the right, 135 knots per sq. in.
*Warp:* wool, 2-ply, "S" spun overall
*Weft:* wool, 2 shoots, 2-ply, "S" spun overall

Figure 2-19. Asymmetric knots open to the left.

Figure 2-20. Asymmetric knot open to the left. Note the tufts emerging from the left of the knot loops. No tufts pass under the loops.
*Provenance:* Qashqai
*Pile:* wool, asymmetric knot open to the left, 52 knots per sq. in.
*Warp:* wool, 2-ply, "S" spun overall
*Weft:* wool, 4 shoots, single, "Z" spun

14

Figure 2-21. Symmetric jufti knot, tied on four warps.

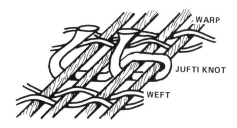

Figure 2-22. Asymmetric jufti knot, tied on four warps.

## Knot density

Knot density is largely determined when the warps are set up on the loom. The number of warps per horizontal inch basically controls knot density.

For coarsely woven rugs the knot count can be as low as 16 per square inch.[1] For finely woven rugs, the knot count has reached 2,000 per square inch in Mughal rugs.[2] Generally, knot density is between 40 and 100 knots per square inch. A density of 100 or more knots per square inch can be considered fine, although fineness of knot density is relative. A knot density of 100 would be considered fine for a Kazak and coarse for a Tabriz.

Usually, vertical knot count is higher than horizontal knot count. Knots are beaten down on the warps with a comb after wefts are woven above the row of knots. This compresses the knot and usually makes it wider than it is high.

Knot count can vary somewhat within the same rug. The knot count can be slightly higher at the bottom of the rug than at the top. Knots may not be beaten down as tightly at the top as the weaver's impatience to finish the rug influences his craftsmanship.

In determining knot density, remember that horizontal knots per inch may be different from vertical knots per inch. Both directions must be counted. If there is little or no warp offset, then two knot nodes per knot are counted in finding the density. However, if warp offset is so great that only a single node of each pair can be seen, then only one node per knot is counted in finding the density.

Figure 2-23. 25 knots per sq. in. No warp offset.
*Provenance:* Kurdish
*Pile:* wool, symmetric knot, 25 knots per sq. in.
*Warp:* wool, 2-ply, "S" spun overall
*Weft:* wool, 2 shoots, single, "S" spun

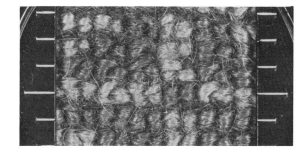

Figure 2-24. 50 knots per sq. in. No warp offset
*Provenance:* Yoruk
*Pile:* wool, symmetric knot, 50 knots per sq. in.
*Warp:* wool, 2-ply, "S" spun overall
*Weft:* wool, 2 to 6 shoots, single, "Z" spun

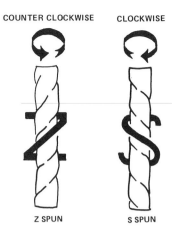

Figure 2-25. 102 knots per sq. in. Very slight warp offset.
*Provenance:* Baluchi
*Pile:* wool, asymmetric knot open to the left, 102 knots per sq. in.
*Warp:* wool, 2-ply, "S" spun overall
*Weft:* wool, 2 shoots, 2 "Z" spun parallel singles

Figure 2-26. Yarn spin. "Z" spun or counter-clockwise and "S" spun or clockwise.

## Yarn spin and ply

When they are made from fiber, yarns are twisted or spun to the left or right. Yarn spun to the left is termed "S" spun and yarn spun to the right is termed "Z" spun.

A yarn that is twisted only once is termed a "single." If two or more singles are twisted together, the combined singles are referred to as a "ply." Two singles make up a two-ply yarn; three singles make up a three-ply yarn, and so on. When yarn singles are plied, they are usually twisted in a direction opposite to the twist of the singles. "Z" spun singles would be "S" plied and "S" spun singles would be "Z" plied.

To complicate matters further, plied yarns can be plied again. For example, if three two-ply yarns are spun together in a direction opposite to the spin of the initial ply, the result is a cord.

For authentic restoration, yarn with the same spin and ply as the original must be used. However, spin and ply matching is not critical for most rug repair.

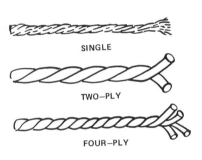

Figure 2-27. Yarn ply.

## Natural fibers used in oriental rugs

A wide variety of natural fibers are used in oriental rugs. By far the most common are wool, cotton and silk. Goat hair, camel hair, horse hair, yak hair and jute are also used.

Some of these fibers can only be distinguished microscopically. With experience, wool, cotton and silk can be identified by their appearance and texture. In comparison to cotton, wool is less soft, more coarsely textured and has more "spring" to it. Undyed cotton has a hard white appearance as compared to white wool. Silk is more flexible and glossier than either wool or cotton, though it's possible to mistake very glossy wool or mercerized cotton for silk.

When in doubt about yarns or fibers, a very small quantity can be burnt. This test is fairly reliable.

Natural sheep wool may be colored brown, fawn, yellow, black and grey, as well as white. The natural colors of wool have been exploited in rug design. This is seen in the so-called "Gaba" rugs of Iran. Naturally colored wool is more often used in weft and warp than in pile.

| Fiber | Odor | Ash | Flame |
|---|---|---|---|
| Wool | Strong odor of burning hair | Forms elongated ball | Barely sustains flame |
| Cotton | Strong odor of burning newspaper | Forms fine ash | Burns easily and brightly |
| Silk | Mild indistinct burning odor | Forms spherical ball | Does not easily sustain flame |

As a group, vegetable fibers are much more resistant to alkalis than animal fibers. Animal fibers will disintegrate in a strong lye solution while vegetable fibers will remain intact. This is one way of distinguishing silk and cotton.

## Wool

The most important qualities in wool are fiber fineness, fiber length and natural color. These qualities are primarily determined by the breed of sheep, but they are also influenced by climate and pasturage.

The fineness of wool fibers ranges from a thickness of 1/3000 inch to 1/275 inch. The merino and its crossbreds regularly produce the finest wool, but fine wool is also taken in the first shearing of lambs from many breeds. Breeds producing coarse wools are generally found in the middle east. Fairly coarse wools have better wear resistance than fine wools.

Wool fibers are covered with microscopic scales. These scales assist fiber adherence in felting and in spinning. Fibers without these scales from pelt-bearing animals are considered hair. In fact, both hair and wool are found on sheep. Coarse hair in wool, called "kemps", is undesirable because it is off color and does not accept dye.

Some wool fibers or staple are as long as 20 inches. Longer staple wool is grown on the shoulders while shorter staple is grown on the rump of the sheep. The length of wool or staple in the fleece makes a difference in commercial yarn production. Wool yarns are classed as woolens or worsteds. Wools of long staple are used in worsted yarns. By combing, the long staple is made to lie parallel before spinning. The result is a stronger, glossier and more flexible yarn. Short staple wools are carded, but fibers are less parallel when they are spun. This produces woolens.

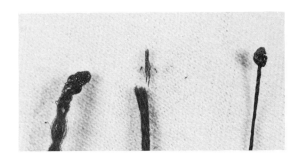

Figure 2-28. Natural fiber ash. On the left is wool ash, in the center is cotton ash and on the right is silk ash.

Worsted yarns are preferred for rug making and rug repair.[3] Worsted yarns used for pile will wear slowly, leaving a paint brush tip. Woolen spun yarns used in pile produce fluff, losing substance and wearing rapidly.

WOOLEN (CARDED)

WORSTED (COMBED)

Figure 2-29. Fiber orientation of woolen yarn and worsted yarn.

## Cotton

The use of cotton in the foundation of pile rugs is a very old practice. There are 17th century Persian carpets with warp and weft of cotton.[4] Indeed, most town or factory rugs have warps of cotton. Undyed cotton is used occasionally for pile in small areas where its hard white appearance provides contrast. Cotton is not generally used as an all-over pile fiber because of its tendency to mat.

Cotton is grown throughout the middle east and Asia. Egyptian cotton is well known for its long staple, only exceeded in length by Georgia Sea Island cotton. Staple length varies from 3/8 inch to 2-1/2 inch, the longer staple being more prized.

Fiber of the cotton plant has the cross-section of a flattened tube. The fiber is naturally twisted, and this characteristic makes it easier to spin.

Mercerized cotton is cotton yarn treated with caustic alkali while the yarn is under tension. This process increases the luster of the yarn to the point where it can be mistaken for silk.

## Silk

Silk is used in the pile and foundation of some of the most costly middle eastern and Chinese rugs. Silk is sometimes used for the pile in a rug with a cotton or wool foundation. In some Turkmen and Caucasian rugs, small colored areas of silk pile are found with an otherwise wool pile.

The principal source of cultivated silk is the cocoon of the moth, *Bombyx mori*. Filament from the cocoon is about 1/1,200 inch in thickness and from 800 to 1,200 yards in length. Commercial silk from cultivated moths is initially classified as reeled or unreeled silk.

Reeled silk is unwound directly from undamaged cocoons floating in a hot water bath. Reeled silk is made up of long parallel filaments before it is spun. This pearly soft-white silk is the finest and most highly valued.

Unreeled or spun silk comes from damaged or stained cocoons. The cocoon filament is loosened by fermentation or washing. After cleaning, the tangled filament is combed and then spun.

Wild or tussur silk, from a variety of moth species, is collected and processed in remote areas of the orient and middle east. Tussur silk is usually grey, but it can be brown or orange depending on the particular moth species. Tussur silk dyes poorly. It is dyed successfully only in darker colors.

## Rug colors

The colors are often included in a technical description of an oriental rug. Unfortunately, these color descriptions are neither precise nor uniform. The designation "brown" is not very enlightening when one considers that the human eye can distinguish about 2,000 colors.[5]

Although a uniform color standard and terminology is of doubtful value in identifying dyes, it would be of great value in comparing and classifying oriental rugs. The Munsell Book of Colors comprises 1,500 color standards with a systematic notation.[6] It would certainly be easier to visualize a specific rug if its technical description employed such a standard system.

Color identification and comparison of oriental rugs is helpful in their study. But, for rug repair, color *description* is less important than the correct color *match* of new repair yarn with original yarn in a rug. Color matching yarns will be discussed in Chapter 4.

## Edge finishes

The edge finish of oriental rugs usually consists of one of these arrangements:

1. A single warp bound by the returning weft.
2. A single warp bound by the returning weft and then overcast.
3. Multiple warps through which the weft is woven (selvage).
4. Multiple warps through which the weft is woven (selvage) and then overcast with one of several figure eight stitches.

The edges of some rugs are overcast in segments of different colors. And rarely, one encounters a rug with tassles or pompoms attached to the edge.

Particular edge finishes are characteristic of certain rug-producing tribes or areas and the original edge is an important identifying feature. Edge finishes are not an entirely reliable guide to a rug's origin because the edges are usually the first areas to show wear. Edges are often repaired and strengthened by overcasting. The material or manner of repair overcasting is likely to differ from the original edge finish. A more detailed discussion of edge structure variations is presented in Chapter 7.

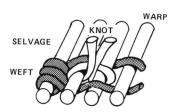

Figure 2-30. A single edge warp bound by the returning weft.

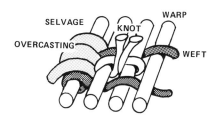

Figure 2-31. A single edge warp bound by the returning weft and then overcast.

Figure 2-32. An edge warp bundle with striped overcasting.
*Provenance:* Qashgai
*Pile:* wool, asymmetric knot open to the left, 63 knots per sq. in.
*Warp:* wool, 2-ply, "S" spun overall
*Weft:* wool, 2 shoots, single "Z" spun

19

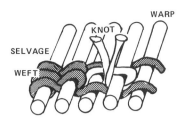

Figure 2-33. Multiple warps through which the weft is woven.

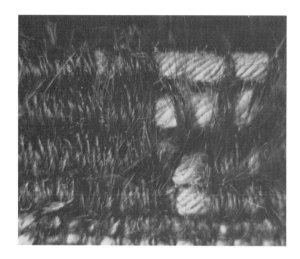

Figure 2-34. Four edge warp bundles through which the weft is woven.
*Provenance:* Baluchi
*Pile:* wool, asymmetric knot open to the left, 56 knots per sq. in.
*Warp:* wool, 2-ply (except for edge warp bundles), "S" spun overall
*Weft:* wool, 2 shoots, single "Z" spun

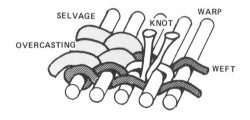

Figure 2-35. Multiple warps through which the weft is woven and then overcast with figure eight stitches.

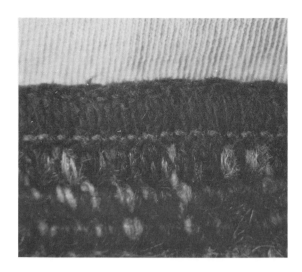

Figure 2-36. Machine overcasting along the edge of a hand knotted rug.
*Provenance:* Kars runner
*Pile:* wool, symmetric knot, 36 knots per sq. in.
*Warp:* wool, 3-ply, "S" spun overall
*Weft:* cotton, 2 to 4 shoots, 2-ply, "S" spun overall

## End finishes

The wefts at the top and bottom ends of a rug are structurally essential. Without them, end knots loosen quickly and the rug begins to unravel. You have probably seen rugs where the end borders have been lost due to this unraveling.

The simplest method of locking the end warps is to weave wefts through the warps to form a heavy fabric at the ends. This is called a killim, flatweave or webbing end. The killim end can be ornamented by using wefts of different colors to create stripes. It can also be ornamented with brocade.

Another method of locking the end warps is to weave in several wefts and then knot the warps together. There are a number of more or less elaborate knotting systems. Some of these systems produce mesh or tassle ends. The knotted tassle end for warps is useful because it stops all unraveling so long as the knots are intact. The killim end with only unknotted warps will unravel if the rug is used.

20

Still another type of end finish is to weave several wefts through the warps and then bind the warps with a chain stitch. A variety of chain stitches are used for this purpose. A more detailed discussion of end finishes is presented in Chapter 8.

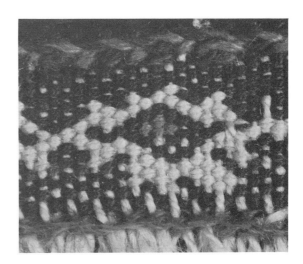

Figure 2-39. End finish. Weft float patterning.
*Provenance:* Baluchi bag face
*Pile:* wool, asymmetric knot open to the left, 99 knots per sq. in.
*Warp:* wool, 2-ply, "S" spun overall
*Weft:* wool, 2 shoots, single, "S" spun overall

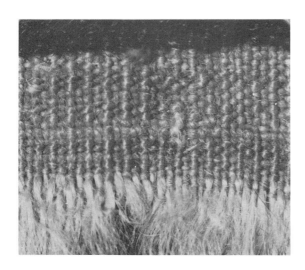

Figure 2-37. End finish. Simple killim end.
*Provenance:* Anatolian yastik
*Pile:* wool, symmetric knot, 104 knots per sq. in.
*Warp:* wool, 2-ply, "S" spun overall
*Weft:* wool, 2 shoots, single, "S" spun

Figure 2-38. End finish. Killim end folded under and sewn.
*Provenance:* Anatolian yastik
*Pile:* wool, symmetric knot, 80 knots per sq. in.
*Warp:* wool, 2-ply, "S" spun overall
*Weft:* wool, 3 shoots, single, "Z" spun

Figure 2-40. End finish. Simple knotting.
*Provenance:* Turkmen (Iranian) prayer rug.
*Pile:* wool, asymmetric knot open to the left, 100 knots per sq. in.
*Warp:* wool, 2-ply, "S" spun overall
*Weft:* wool, 3 shoots, single, "S" spun

Figure 2-41. End finish. Macramé.
*Provenance:* Kuba
*Pile:* wool, symmetric knot, 112 knots per sq. in.
*Warp:* wool, 3-ply, "S" spun overall
*Weft:* wool, 2 shoots, single, "S" spun

Figure 2-42. End finish. Braided.
*Provenance:* Hamadan runner
*Pile:* wool, symmetric knot, 63 knots per sq. in.
*Warp:* cotton, single, "S" spun
*Weft:* cotton, 1 shoot, single "S" spun

Figure 2-43. End finish. Braided.
*Provenance:* Kazak
*Pile:* wool, symmetric knot, 33 per sq. in.
*Warp:* wool, 2-ply, "S" spun overall
*Weft:* wool, 2 to 8 shoots, single, "Z" spun

## Technical analysis and repair

Technical analysis is an essential tool in positively classifying oriental rugs, the key to determining a rug's rarity and value. But, more importantly, the ability to analyze rug structure is a prerequisite to repair.

To develop that ability, form the habit of looking at rugs critically. Regularly identify these structural features when you examine a rug:

1. Pile material
2. Knot type
3. Approximate knot density
4. Number of wefts between rows of knots
5. Warp material
6. Warp offset
7. Edge and end finish

All of these features, plus color, must be matched in rug repair. Finally, learn about the rugs you repair - their origin, age and typical structural features. This knowledge will help assure that your repairs are appropriate and tasteful.

1. Kendrick and Tattersall, *Hand Woven Carpets,* Dover, 1973, p.97

2. W. B. Denny, *Oriental Rugs,* Smithsonian Institution, 1979, p.107

3. P. Collingwood, *The Techniques of Rug Weaving* Watson-Guptill Publications, 1978. p.61

4. M. B. Lanier, *English and Oriental Carpets at Williamsburg,* The Colonial Williamsburg Foundation, 1975, p.16

5. R. Pinner, *The Role of Scientific Techniques in Carpet Studies,* Hali, Vol. II No. 1, 1979, p.20, 21

6. *Color—Universal Language and Dictionary of Names,* U.S. Dept. of Commerce, 1976, p.A-13

# Chapter 3

# Damage to Oriental Rugs

The Pazyrk carpet, discovered in an ancient grave in Siberia, has survived for 2,500 years. That's an amazing endurance record for a pile rug. But then it was frozen for most of the time. It was not exposed to wear, insect attack and rot—the sources of damage that often bring a 25-year old rug to the scrap heap.

Ultimately, protection from damage depends on the owner's view of the rug's value, for this determinnes how well he or she will care for the rug. The value of oriental rugs has varied with fashions in interior decoration. When oriental rugs were out of fashion, their value declined and they received less care. Accordingly, the techniques of repair could be considered as remedies for failures in popular judgment as to what is beautiful, valuable, and thus worth preserving. This survey of damage to oriental rugs explains the variety of problems we must solve in preserving a rug through techniques of repair and restoration.

**Wear in the field**

For some oriental rug buyers, moderate wear increases the desirability of the rug. Wear softens colors and sometimes increases the gloss of the pile as very fine fibers are worn away.

There are several distinct stages of wear in the field:

1. Pile height varies due to wear, but knot loops are concealed.

2. Knot loops are visible from the front of the rug.

3. The foundation is exposed; warp and weft are visible.

Often, all three stages are seen in the same worn area.

Variation in pile height due to wear is a normal condition in rugs and reknotting merely to even pile height is not justified so long as knot loops and foundation are concealed.

Where knot loops are exposed, reknotting may or may not be desirable. If the area with exposed knot loops is small and contrasts with the rest of the rug, then reknotting the area to make it consistent in appearance with the surrounding pile is probably desirable. If the area with exposed knot loops is large, then reknotting the area is probably not justified unless the rug is very valuable.

Figure 3-1. A rug worn to the foundation. Note the exposed warp and weft. The knot loops are visible in most areas.
*Provenance:* Kuba
*Pile:* wool, symmetric knot, 60 knots per sq. in.
*Warp:* wool, 2-ply, "S" spun overall
*Weft:* wool, 2 shoots, 2-ply, "S" spun overall

In general, where the foundation is exposed, the area should be reknotted. If the exposed foundation is surrounded by an area of exposed knot loops, which, in turn is surrounded by an area of full pile, then the repairer has a choice. The new knots over the exposed foundation can be clipped to expose the knot loop or the new pile can hide the knot loop. Usually, it is best to clip the new pile down to the knot loop in this situation. A more natural and consistent appearance results. If full pile is left in the reknotted area, then all knots with exposed loops should be replaced. In any case, the goal is

consistency in appearance rather than contrast in pile height or knot exposure.

It is easiest to blend a reknotted area into the surrounding rug under these conditions:

1. The reknotted area is relatively small.

2. Surrounding pile is long rather than short or worn.

3. The reknotted area is in a multi-colored portion of the rug rather than in a large single colored area.

4. The reknotted area consists of dark rather than light colors.

**Edge wear**

Wear to rug edges is probably the most common type of wear. In a typical rug, wear at the edge proceeds in these stages:

1. Overcasting is worn away exposing weft loops.

2. Weft loops wear away.

3. Edge warps loosen from the rug.

4. Edge warps wear through and break.

Clearly, much damage is avoided if repair overcasting is done in time to prevent broken wefts or warps. Overcasting is a simple repair though it can be slighty complicated by multiple edge warps in the selvage.

If a number of adjacent weft loops wear away, then wefts must be restored to bind selvage warps to the rug. This greatly increases the time and effort of repair.

Where warps have parted these must be restored. The rug edge is mounted on a frame to keep the edge under tension during repair. Otherwise, restored warps and edge will not be straight when repairs are completed. Where warps are restored, then weft and overcasting are restored, as well.

24

Wear sufficient to part the warps usually exposes the foundation near the edge. Reknotting may be needed in this case.

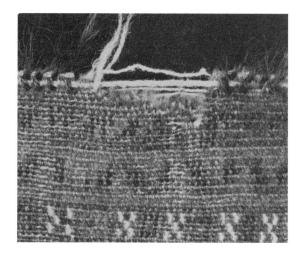

Figure 3-2. A broken selvage. The damage extends into the rug where weft and knots are lost.
*Provenance:* Baluchi
*Pile:* wool, asymmetric knot open to the left, 48 knots per sq. in.
*Warp:* wool, 2-ply, "S" spun overall
*Weft:* wool, 3 shoots, 2 parallel singles each "Z" spun

## Wear at the ends

Oriental pile rugs are framed by the main border and guard stripes. We are used to this frame; it suggests completeness. Without guard stripes and main border, the rug seems unfinished. And this is the impression created when guard stripes or borders are lost through wear and damage to the ends of the rug.

These are the stages of wear at the ends:

1. Knotted warps in the fringe unravel.

2. Killim wefts unravel.

3. Wear proceeds quickly into the pile knots, then guard stripes and border are lost.

Costly reconstruction or compromise repairs are avoided if end repair is done in time to save the pile knots.

One treatment of damaged ends is to pull out incomplete wefts and pile knots to square off the end of the rug. Then, the remaining full wefts are locked in place by reknotting the warp, whip stitching into the rug, or chain stitching along the end. These measures are usually satisfactory if the guard stripes and border in the pile are left intact. However, if squaring the end requires the loss of a guard stripe or border, the result usually appears awkward and unfinished.

Figure 3-3. Loss of the border at the end. Compare the complete top end with the incomplete bottom end.
*Provenance:* Yastik
*Pile:* wool, symmetric knot, 75 knots per sq. in.
*Warp:* wool, 2-ply, "S" spun overall
*Weft:* wool, 3 to 4 shoots, single, "Z" spun

If the rug is sufficiently valuable, reconstruction of the damaged area is the best approach. However, this is one of the more difficult repairs. The warps and killim end strip must be reconstructed before reknotting is done at the bottom. Reconstruction of killim end strips is complicated if they are brocaded or ornamented in some other way. Of course, the repairer may choose to reconstruct the end strip without restoring ornamentation.

## Holes through the foundation

Holes through the foundation are time-consuming to repair by reconstruction. The repair time required increases with the knot density and the size of the hole. The loss of pile knots and warps occurs quickly once there is a break in the warps. So, for a rug in use, the sooner the hole is repaired, the less costly the repair.

As the prices of oriental rugs continue to rise, older and more extensively damaged pieces will be repaired. Rugs that were not believed to merit the repair investment will be re-evaluated in view of current rug prices. Some of these rugs will have previous repairs that were unsatisfactorily done. These will include compromise repairs of holes through the foundation.

One such compromise is to sew up or darn the hole. This may spoil the design from the front of the rug, especially if the pile is short or the hole is large.

Sometimes a patch is taken from a scrap rug and sewn into the hole. This is called a "plug". Usually, there is a mismatch in design and color with a plug.

Yet another approach is to sew a patch of coarse fabric, of the type used for hooked rugs, to the back of the rug over the hole. This fabric provides the warp base for re-knotting in colors and design to match the rug. Of the compromise repairs for holes, this last one is probably most acceptable for relatively inexpensive rugs that will be returned to use.

The best repair for holes is to reconstruct warp and weft and reknot. For rugs of moderate or finer knot densities, this tends to be a large repair investment justified only for fairly valuable or rare rugs.

Figure 3-4. Hole through the foundation.
*Provenance:* Salor
*Pile:* wool, asymmetric knot open to the right, 152 knots per sq. in.
*Warp:* wool, 2-ply, "Z" spun overall
*Weft:* wool, 2 shoots, single, "Z" spun

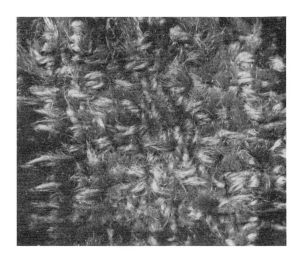

Figure 3-5. A hole that has been darned. This is an unsatisfactory compromise.
*Provenance:* Salor
*Pile:* wool, asymmetric knot open to the right, 152 knots per sq. in.
*Warp:* wool, 2-ply, "Z" spun overall
*Weft:* wool, 2 shoots, single, "Z" spun

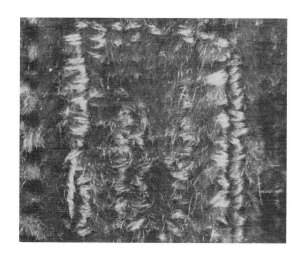

Figure 3-6. A hole patched with a piece from another rug. This use of a "plug" is an unsatisfactory compromise.
*Provenance:* Salor
*Pile:* wool, asymmetric knot open to the right, 152 knots per sq. in.
*Warp:* wool, 2-ply, "Z" spun overall
*Weft:* wool, 2 shoots, single, "Z" spun

## Tears and cuts

Tears are across the warps, across the wefts or across both warp and weft. Tears occur when the foundation is weakened by wear or rot or the foundation is subjected to exceptional mechanical stress.

Torn or parted warps must be reconstructed before reknotting. For warp repairs, the repair area is supported by a frame. This assures warps will be under equal tension as repairs proceed, preventing wrinkles or distortions in the foundation. Needle movement in warp repair is usually slow and difficult because the needle is forced through existing knots. The value of the rug should justify this repair investment.

There is a special case of warp restoration where runners have been cut to shorten them. Each oriental rug is designed as a totality. Both pattern and structure are intended to remain as a whole throughout the rug's life. When the beauty and craftsmanship of oriental rugs were less respected,

runners were sometimes cut down to fit them to available space. A piece was removed from the runner and the end re-attached by sewing and sometimes by gluing.

These altered runners are now showing up for permanent repair through reconstruction. This reconstruction requires work on edges or selvages, warp restoration, weft restoration and reknotting. Once again, the final value of the runner is the first consideration in deciding whether this repair investment is worthwhile.

Tears across the wefts are somewhat easier to repair than warp tears. Weft tears are most likely to occur between two columns of knots, since the knots provide lateral strength to each knotted pair of warps. Needle movement is not so slow in weft restoration because wefts lie between the knots.

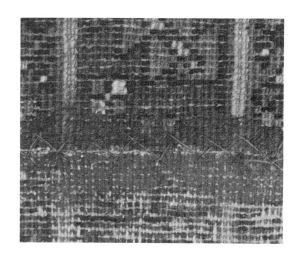

Figure 3-7. A shortened runner. The two pieces have been sewn and glued together.
*Provenance:* Karabaugh runner
*Pile:* wool, symmetric knot, 56 knots per sq. in.
*Warp:* cotton, 5-ply, "S" spun overall
*Weft:* cotton, 2-shoots, 3-ply, "S" spun overall

Figure 3-8. A cross-weft tear. Warps are separated primarily between columns of knots.
*Provenance:* Anatolian prayer rug
*Pile:* wool, symmetric knot, 36 knots per sq. in.
*Warp:* wool, 2-ply, "S" spun overall
*Weft:* wool, 3 shoots, 3-ply, "S" spun overall

Figure 3-9. Moth damage. The wool pile is eaten away and the cotton foundation remains.
*Provenance:* Karabaugh runner
*Pile:* wool, symmetric knot, 56 knots per sq. in.
*Warp:* cotton, 5-ply, "S" spun overall
*Weft:* cotton, 2 shoots, 3-ply, "S" spun overall

## Insect damage

The primary culprits are the clothes moth, *Tineola bisseliella*, and the black carpet beetle, *Attagenus piceus*. These insects, in their larva state, have an appetite for the keratin in natural hair and wool fibers. They will eat through other fibers to get to animal fibers.

The adult clothes moth is about one-half inch long, not to be confused with larger moths. As a larva, it increases its original weight 300 times. If each of about 90 eggs laid by the female moth actually hatch, a host·rug can be devastated. The larvae of the carpet beetle are about one-quarter inch long, while the adult beetle is about half that size.[1]

These insects prefer soiled animal fiber. So a preventive measure is to keep rugs clean. Since they also prefer darkness, rugs in storage are more vulnerable than rugs in use. To place a soiled rug in storage is to invite insect damage.

The larvae devour wool and eschew cotton. As a result, their damage to a wool pile cotton foundation rug is characteristic. The wool disappears in patches while the foundation remains intact. Simple reknotting solves the problem. This is one of the most successful repairs. In all-wool rugs, holes will penetrate the foundation and insect damage is more costly to repair.

## Mildew and rot

Mildew is fungi. The growth of fungi may be visible on a rug as a mould or its growth can remain invisible to the naked eye. Damage to fibers can occur in either case. Fungi produce filaments or "hyphae". These penetrate natural fibers and break them down, producing rot.[2]

Both cotton and wool are susceptible to mildew and rot, but cotton is especially vulnerable. Fungi thrive on the cellulose in cotton.

After a cotton foundation has been exposed to serious mildew or rot, it loses strength and becomes brittle. The condition is irreversible. Cracking or creaking when a rug is bent is the telltale sound of rot. A rug can be tested for rot by starting a fold at the top of the rug and working the fold down the length of the rug so the whole rug passes through the fold. By listening carefully for a cracking sound, one can identify specific areas of rot.

Rot is acceptable if a rug is to be displayed only. A rotted rug in use will disintegrate quickly. There is no point in investing repair effort in a rug with widespread rot. Conservation or protection from mechanical stress are the only reasonable measures. The total extent of rot should be found before any repairs are attempted. If rot is limited to small areas, the rotted material can be cut out and the area reconstructed. This is justified only if the rug is sufficiently valuable.

Figure 3-10. Mildew of cotton wefts. The knots hold pairs of wool warps together.
*Provenance:* Kurdish runner
*Pile:* wool, symmetric knot, 49 knots per sq. in.
*Warp:* wool, 3-ply, "S" spun overall
*Weft:* cotton, 3 shoots, 2-ply, "S" spun overall

Since cotton is used in the foundation and cotton is more susceptible to rot than wool, the effect of rot depends on how the cotton is used. If both warp and weft are cotton, then the rotted foundation will disintegrate. If only wefts are cotton and warps are wool, then only the wefts will rot and disintegrate. This may produce the slit effect shown in the accompanying illustration.

Fungi grow in humid or wet conditions. Warmth and darkness foster growth. The ultra-violet rays of sunlight arrest or discourage mildew. Consequently, rugs in storage must be kept dry. If rugs are stored in a humid atmosphere, they should be aired in the sunlight periodically to prevent the growth of mildew.

### Wrinkles and curls

Occasionally, one finds a rug that won't lie flat. When looms are not rigid or warps vary in tension across the loom, wrinkles can be woven into the rug. This is more likely to occur with nomadic or village rugs than with factory or city rugs.

The cost of removing wrinkles by cutting a wedge out of the rug and then reweaving and reknotting is practically never justified. If a wrinkle cannot be removed by steam pressing, it's best to view the wrinkle as a sign of hand craftsmanship, just as design inconsistencies and abrash are viewed.

Humid weather may cause some rugs to wrinkle or curl because of their natural fiber content. For example, the goat hair used in the foundation of south Ersari rugs causes the corners to curl in a distinctive manner.[3] Edges of a rug may curl under when weft is drawn too tightly.

Steam pressing is sometimes effective,in removing wrinkles and curls. After a rug is washed and rinsed, it can be stretched to remove wrinkles and curls by nailing the rug, down as it dries. This approach may be successful in some cases.

Figure 3-11. Curled corner on a rug with goat hair warps.
*Provenance:* Ersari ensi
*Pile:* wool, asymmetric knot open to the left, 56 knots per sq. in.
*Warp:* goat hair, 2-ply, "S" spun overall
*Weft:* wool, 2 shoots, single, "Z" spun

Figure 3-12. Etching. In this example, black areas are etched to the foundation while light colored areas still retain pile.

## Etching or corrosion

No acid is involved, only certain dyes, wear and time. An older rug that has a consistently lowered pile in areas of the same color is etched. The effect is unlike the "sculptured" pile in Chinese rugs, which usually has a molded appearance. In etching, there is a sharp difference in pile height between etched colors and unaffected colors. The relief may not be great but it *is* sharp. Slight etching is most evident in a raking light or a low visual angle.

Etching occurs when certain non-commercial dyes containing metallic salts weaken the wool fibers. Through wear, these fibers break down more quickly than other fibers. In time, the affected areas may be worn down to the knot or foundation while pile in other colors is full.

The colors most liable to etching when dyed are black and brown. A single row of knots in an etched color looks like a channel running through the pile. In a rug where different adjacent colors have etched, the pile can take on a terraced appearance.

From this description, you might suspect that etching is a fault that lowers the value of the rug. Generally, this is not the case. Etching may be viewed as a mark of authenticity. The rug is probably old and colored with vegetable dyes at a time before commercial dyes were available to the weaver.

Because etching is viewed as a sign of age, counterfeiters have been known to clip the black or brown pile in newer rugs to simulate etching.[4] Since moderate etching adds to the value of a rug, re-knotting etched areas is normally appropriate only when etching has exposed the foundation of the rug. Certainly, the warp and weft must be protected by pile if the rug is to be used.

## Fading and washing

The ultraviolet component of sunlight is responsible for most color fading in rugs. Different dyes react in a different manner to sunlight so that fading is not usually consistent across the hues in a rug. Fading is the normal consequence of use and wear and usually affects the front of the rug more than the back.

The difference in depth of color between front and back due to normal fading cannot be specified exactly. However, this difference should be moderate. If colors on the front of the rug are mellow and the colors on the back are bright and harsh, then another process may have been at work: washing.

"Washing" is the deliberate use of chemical bleaches to soften the colors in a rug. The whole rug may be washed, or only the front. If strong bleaches were used, the fiber may be severely weakened. Sometimes rugs are washed and then touched up with dyes to brighten certain colors. This has been done with many Sarouks. There is no remedy for the harmful effects of a strong chemical wash.

How can you tell whether a rug has faded normally or been washed? For an all-over wash, this cannot be done reliably outside of a laboratory. When only the front has been washed, there are a couple of clues. There will be a high contrast between front and back colors. Since wear usually accompanies normal fading, a color contrast between front and back in rugs where the pile shows little or no wear makes the rug suspect.

In an older rug, an area that has been re-knotted using different wool and dyes is likely to fade at a different rate than adjacent areas. If this has occurred and the contrast is offensive, then reknotting with a closer color match is the best solution.

## Stains

Because of their size and use in high traffic areas, rugs are subject to a wider variety of staining substances than most household fabrics. The pile makes rugs more absorbent than other fabrics and complicates the removal of some substances. Wool does not have the resistance to stains possessed by many synthetic fibers. This is the same quality that makes wool relatively easy to color with natural or vegetable dyes.

Stains are unwanted substances that are not removable by normal washing. This does not mean that you should wait until the rug is washed to identify and remove stains. Any substance that *may* stain should be removed immediately. This prevents the stain from spreading, and, more importantly, prevents the stain from fixing or permanently setting through the passage of time. Stains can also be set by using the wrong procedures or solvents in attempting to remove them. Actual stain removal procedures, staining substances and appropriate solvents are discussed in Chapter 9.

## Painting

Usually, "painting" is coloring areas of a rug that have been worn to the foundation. This is done to match the surrounding pattern and colors. At a glance, these areas appear to be covered with pile. Small painted areas are likely to be overlooked by the unsuspecting buyer. The buyer soon becomes a skeptic if the rug is cleaned and the colors wash away or run. Rapidly climbing rug prices and the prevalence of colored felt tip pens have fostered this type of forgery. Clearly, a "painted rug" is the antithesis of "dyed in the wool."

Painting rugs is not a new invention. In the 1920's, some new Sarouks imported into the United States were first bleached to soften colors and then the pile of the field was painted with dyes to produce a rich maroon. Dealers in Iran sometimes have the pile of new rugs painted with dye if they find certain colors unacceptable.

A painted foundation does not preclude re-knotting. However, if the colors used on the foundation are not fast, they will bleed into lighter areas of re-knotted pile. Painted areas should be tested for color fastness before re-knotting. This is done by moistening a piece of clean white cloth with a weak solution of detergent and water. With the cloth, briskly rub the painted area. If the cloth picks up any color, then re-knotting in light colors is not practical unless the painted colors can be washed out or fixed permanently.

## Reknotting in a different color— aesthetics versus ethics

Suppose someone brings you a rug for minor reknotting. The rug is not especially valuable. "Oh yes, and while you're reknotting the bald spots, would you reknot these small pink areas in tan yarn so they match the color of the field?"

Sometimes a rug that is otherwise subtle or harmonious in color will sport a dash of magenta, hot pink, harsh orange or electric blue. Reknot or not? That's the question.

A connoisseur may argue that an oriental rug is a work of art. To change the colors, no matter how slightly, violates the artist's intentions. A change of color would be a crime against art no less than bowdlerizing statuary with fig leaves where the artist had been true to nature.

But are *all* oriental rugs works of art? Only in the sense they are hand made. Certainly, there are rugs that are poorly woven, garishly colored with ugly designs. These are not works of art. They are only floor coverings. What is the distinction between a rug that is a work of art and one that is merely a floor covering? The answer depends on your own definition of art. Usually, the answer is a personal judgment.

There's the anthropological argument against changing colors. An oriental rug is a cultural artifact that should be preserved as such. Accordingly, it's wrong to modify a product of Near-eastern culture to suit twentieth-century Western tastes.

The fact is that most oriental rugs presently in European and American homes were intended to appeal to Western tastes. Most of these rugs were made for export to Western markets. Relatively few of these rugs are cultural expressions untempered by Western influence. Knowledge of the origins and age of oriental rugs is your only guide in deciding what rugs are trade goods and what rugs were intended by their weavers for local use. If you adopt the anthropological point of view, you will not change the colors in rugs that weavers wove for themselves.

Bad chemistry has altered the color of some rugs. Due to unstable aniline dyes, a magenta may have turned brown or a green turned grey. More raucous color changes are possible. Time can create discords in the harmonious palette originally selected by the weaver. In such cases, is reknotting in the original color or a more harmonious color acceptable?

We have no definite answer to the aesthetic and ethical questions raised by reknotting areas of an oriental rug to change their color. You must decide the issue for yourself.

## Surveying the damage

Before any actual repairs are begun on a rug, it's a good idea to identify *all* the damage. A way to do this is to mark the damage by making long stitches around each repair area with thread of a contrasting color. Then, you can look at the whole rug and form a reasonable estimate of the total amount of work to be done. This could affect your decision as to whether you want to do *any* work on the rug. Marking damaged areas serves to emphasize the extent of repairs to the owner of the rug and prevents you from overlooking damaged areas when repairs are in progress.

1. J.R. McPhee *The Mothproofing of Wool*, Merrow, 1971 p.4,5

2. M. Bogle, *Textile Dyes, Finishes and Auxiliaries*, Garland Publishing, Inc. 1977, p.104,105

3. W.B. Denny, *Oriental Rugs*, The Smithsonian Institute, 1979, p.98

4. U. Schurman, *Oriental Carpets*, Octopus Books, 1979, p.35

# Chapter 4

# Selecting Yarn

When selecting yarns for rug repairs, the goal is to match the existing yarn exactly. In practice, this goal is almost unattainable. Yarns are just not available in sufficient variety. Even though one must compromise, at a minimum, these characteristics should be matched:

- Fiber type
- Color
- Size

The following yarn characteristics are more difficult to match, but consider them when you select yarns:

- Quality (glossiness, coarseness, staple length)
- Spin, ply and tightness of twist

Color match is probably the most critical judgment you'll make in selecting yarns for repairs. Mismatched color quickly draws attention to structural inconsistencies in repairs that would otherwise pass unnoticed.

## Components of color

In discussing yarn color, it's helpful to understand the qualities that define a color. These are hue, shade and vividness.[1] *Hues* are the colors of the spectrum and their combinations: red, orange, yellow, green, blue, purple, and brown. The *shade* of a color is determined by the presence of black, white or greys in the color. *Vividness* is the *amount* of black, white or greys in the color. A vivid color has no admixture of black, white or grey. It is a pure hue or combination of hues.

Here's how these definitions apply to red. Red is the hue. By mixing red and black, we produce the dark shade of maroon. By mixing red and white we produce the light shade of pink. Pink and maroon are more or less vivid depending on the amount of white, black or grey they contain. The total absence of white, black or grey produces vivid red.

## Guidelines for color matching

Here are a few guidelines to help you match colors more successfully:

- The rug must be clean, otherwise there is no hope for a good color match. Anyone who has washed rugs knows something of the great color difference between a clean and soiled rug.

- If possible, use yarn color cards to identify the colors of repair yarns. Color cards are provided by yarn suppliers (See "Yarn suppliers"). The color cards identify colors and show the range of yarn colors offered by the supplier by means of samples. For the larger yarn selections, yarn samples of the same hue are mounted on cards together with gradations of shade within the hue. Since you can't bring a large rug into a yarn shop, the color cards are a great help. With color cards, color matching can be done patiently and in the proper light.

- Compare colors in sunlight. This is not essential but very desireable. Next best to sunlight is strong incandescent light. Flourescent light is the least satisfactory.

- Be especially cautious in matching light colors. Whites and yellows are most difficult to match exactly.

- For pile, selvage and overcasting, color comparisons should be made from the front of the rug. Fading may have produced color differences between the front and back of the rug.

## Matching pile color

The color of the same yarn appears lighter if the side of the yarn is viewed than if the cut end of the yarn is viewed. More light is absorbed by the fiber ends, making the color darker. This effect is seen in rugs. A rug is darker and more richly colored when viewed from the bottom, looking into the pile.

Figure 4-1. Some typical examples of yarn color cards.

There's a message here in selecting yarn for pile repairs. When comparing yarn to a rug to match pile yarn colors, hold several cut ends of the yarn sample next to the yarn in the pile. Looking into the pile, compare the color of sample yarn ends with pile yarn ends. Never select pile repair yarn by comparing the side of the yarn sample with the pile.

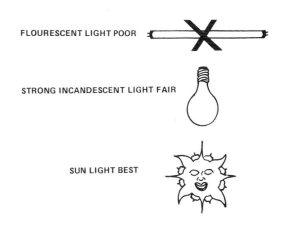

Figure 4-2. Use sunlight for color comparisons whenever possible.

34

Figure 4-3. Matching pile color. Note that cut yarn ends are compared with pile ends.

Matching pile colors includes matching existing abrash, but not adding to it. Abrash is a change in the color of field and border due to differences in the weaver's wool or dye batches. Although abrash can add interest, charm and authenticity to a rug, there's a risk of calling attention to repaired areas if new abrash is introduced through poor color matching. Abrash is more likely to occur at the top of a rug than the bottom. Due to misjudgment or accident, yarn batches of specific colors are used up as the rug nears completion. Then, new batches must be used to finish the rug.

## Matching warp, weft and overcasting color

Because warp, weft and overcasting are viewed from the side of the yarn rather than the end (as is pile), they are color matched with a side-by-side sample comparison.

Appropriate warp color match is especially desirable in end repairs because warps are exposed at the ends. Usually, there's no problem in matching white cotton warps. But where natural coarse wool or goat hair is used for warps, color and texture matching is more difficult. For naturally colored warps, the color may range between black,

brown and grey within the same rug. Some yarn suppliers offer coarse natural wool yarns. See "Yarn suppliers." These are useful in matching warp colors for tribal, nomadic and village rugs. In some tribal rugs, warps are barber-pole striped. These warps can be reproduced by blending and spinning yarns by methods described later in this chapter.

Ground weft color matching is fairly easy because of limited weft visibility and limited weft color range. Whites, browns, greys, reds, blues and black are usually the only colors found in ground wefts. Selvage wefts may be differently colored than ground wefts and create special decorative effects. Color matching, here is just as important as it is in pile color matching.

Color matching for overcasting is straight forward except where coarse natural wool is used. Natural wool yarns or blended yarns may be needed for proper overcasting color match. In comparing yarn for overcasting, wrap your yarn sample around a pencil. Then hold it next to the existing overcasting.

Figure 4-4. Striped or barber pole warp. Sometimes striped warps are used as markers to guide the location of the rug pattern.
*Provenance:* Baluchi
*Pile:* wool, asymmetric knot open to the left, 91 knots per sq. in.
*Warp:* wool, 2-ply, "S" spun overall
*Weft:* wool, 2 shoots, parallel singles, each "Z" spun

35

Figure 4-5. Matching overcasting color. Compare the yarn on the pencil with the selvage overcasting.

## Color matching by blending singles

A yarn produced by a single twisting of the fiber is called a "singles" yarn. Two singles make a two-ply yarn, four singles make a four-ply yarn and so on.[2]

Commercial yarns can usually be untwisted to separate singles or pairs of singles. Singles of differently shaded yarns can be re-combined to make a blend. This capacity to blend singles of different shades gives you the palette of Seurat if not of Rembrandt.

In blending singles the shades vary but the hue must be the same, all blues or all browns, for example. Blending singles works best when the color you wish to match falls between two available shades of yarn, one darker than the desired shade and one lighter than the desired shade. The closer the available yarns are to the desired color, the more successful the blend will be. If the available shades are far apart, then the resulting pile will have a flecked or pepper and salt appearance. If the available yarns closely bracket the desired shade, then the blend can be detected only by very close inspection.

More than two singles can be blended, such as a single of one shade and two or more singles of another shade. It's not necessary to re-twist the singles for pile yarn. They need only be threaded together through the eye of a tapestry needle for use in reknotting.

## Darkening yarns with tea

Tea can be used to darken light colored yarns. This works best if only a small batch of darkened yarn is needed. Brew some tea, the stronger the tea the darker the shade it produces. Immerse the yarn in the hot tea for fifteen minutes. Let the yarn dry. Then wash the yarn three times, drying the yarn after each washing. This washing is important since decreasing amounts of the tea stain are washed out each time. Only the dye remaining after the third washing is permanent.

The results of this dye process are unreliable and difficult to reproduce. That's why it's recommended only for small batches. Experiment with samples before darkening any large batch of yarn with tea.

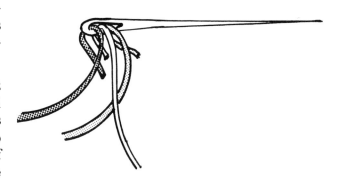

Figure 4-6. Singles of different shades are blended in the needle to create the desired color.

## Why dyeing is difficult

Dyeing is a skill in itself. It's very difficult to get predictable and consistent results without a great deal of experience. There are simply too many variables to control. These variables include:

- Type and quality of dye
- Quality of wool
- Type of mordant (conditions fiber to take up dye)
- Mineral content of water
- Temperature of dye bath and mordant
- Time in dye bath and mordant

Even the pot used for the dye bath can influence results. The tin from a tin-lined copper pot will affect the final color. If worn areas of the pot allow trace amounts of copper into the dye bath, a different shade will be produced. Unless you want to spend a considerable amount of time experimenting with dyes, it's much easier to match rug colors with available commercial yarns.

## Matching size and density of pile yarn

To match the size and density of yarn in the pile, examine a tuft of pile closely. Pull a tuft of worn pile from the rug. It will be kinked and flattened. Not surprising after years of service. Because it's flattened, the tuft may appear larger in diameter than it actually is. Look at the back of the rug and note the average size of the yarn in the knots. Here, again, appearances can be deceptive. Since knots have spread with time, the yarn is not as thick as it seems to be. Feel the back of the rug to form an impression of the relation between knot density and yarn size.

If your new yarn does not match the pile yarn in size or density (more than likely), pull singles or pairs of singles from the new yarn and loosely combine them. Experiment with singles or pairs of singles until your test sample equals the size and density of the pile yarn in the rug. Then, use the same number of singles when you thread your tapestry needle.

Pile yarn is very loosely twisted. So, you don't have to twist the yarn used to reknot pile. It can hang loosely from the needle. The yarn will compact when you draw the knot tight. After the knot is tied, compare it to other knots to make sure the size and density is the same.

For the inexperienced, there's a tendency to use too much yarn in the pile. If the size or density of pile yarn is too large, then the space between warps and the space between wefts will be packed too tightly. As a result, the reknotted area may be stiff or even distorted.

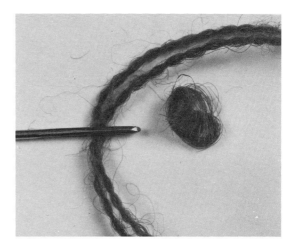

Figure 4-7. A tuft of pile pulled from the rug compared to the yarn that will be used for reknotting.

## Matching size and density of warp and weft

Both warp and weft are normally more tightly spun and stronger than yarns used for the pile. Frequently, warp is larger in size than available Persian or tapestry yarns so some other type of yarn must be used in repairs. In matching warp yarn for repair, a slightly smaller size for the replacement yarn is acceptable, since this will make the reweaving process a little easier and create less distortion in the repair area. Examine the warp in the rug ends close to the foundation when determining warp size because exposed loose warp ends will have untwisted and expanded.

Figure 4-8. The warp in the fringe has expanded or "relaxed" as it extends from the wefts. Compare warp size in the foundation and not at the fringe ends.
*Provenance:* Baluchi
*Pile:* wool, asymmetric knot open to the left, 59 knots per sq. in.
*Warp:* wool, 2-ply, "S" spun overall
*Weft:* wool, 2 shoots, parallel singles, each "Z" spun

Examine the weft in the foundation from the back of the rug. If there is no overcasting and foundation wefts extend into the selvage, then weft size comparison can be made at the selvage; weft in the foundation may be slightly compressed because of the way knots are packed against it during weaving.

There may be some local variation in the size and density of warp and weft within the rug. So it's best to make comparisons in the actual repair area, as well.

### How to re-spin yarns for warp or weft

The yarns available for tapestry work, knitting, crewel or crochet work are not twisted tightly enough for warp and weft and do not usually match the diameter and density of warp or weft in the rug. The tighter twist of warp and weft yarns make them denser, stronger and less fuzzy than most available wool commercial yarns. But, you can make yarn of almost any diameter and degree of twist from available yarns.

Yarns can be easily twisted or re-spun in lengths of a yard or more by using a spindle in much the same way yarns were originally spun for tribal and nomadic rugs. For our purposes, the spindle consists of a piece of one inch diameter lead pipe about four inches in length. A single yarn to be respun or several yarns to be spun together are tied to the center of the pipe. The other end of the yarn is tied to a crosspiece so the spindle is suspended by the yarn. The yarn is thoroughly moistened with water and then the pipe length is spun with a movement of the hand. When the yarn is sufficiently twisted, the pipe length is braced against some object so the yarn remains under tension but cannot untwist. After about one hour, the yarn will be dry. When it is cut from the spindle it will not untwist.

A little experimentation with this method demonstrates the way twist angle affects yarn quality and strength. Color blends for warp and weft can also be made in this manner.

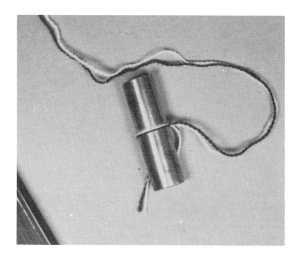

Figure 4-9. Two pieces of yarn attached to the weight before respinning.

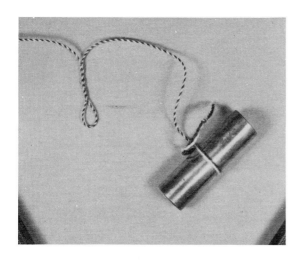

Figure 4-10. Yarn on the weight after re-spinning.

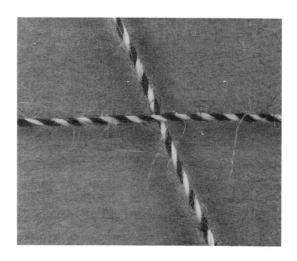

Figure 4-11. The respun yarn.

## Commercial specification of yarns

Commercial specification of yarns is confusing for two reasons. First, the manufacture of yarns is a very old industry and long-standing traditions of different countries have prevented the adoption of a simple international system of yarn description. Secondly, some of the yarns that interest us in rug repair are not standard commercial products and are therefore neither packaged nor labeled in the same way as large sales volume fiber products.

smaller the yarn size. The standard lengths (size 1) for the different fibers are shown in the following table:

A size 2 yarn contains twice the standard length in one pound of yarn, a size 3 yarn contains three times the standard length in one pound of yarn, and so on. For example size 1 worsted yarn contains 560 yards to a pound, size 2 contains 1,120 yards to a pound, size 3 contains 1,680 yards to a pound, and so on. As another example, size 10 cotton yarn would contain 8,400 yards in one pound of yarn.

| FIBER TYPE | SIZE | STANDARD LENGTH | STANDARD QUANTITY |
|---|---|---|---|
| Woolen yarn (carded mixed staple) | 1 | 1,600 yards | One pound of yarn |
| Worsted yarn (combed long staple) | 1 | 560 yards | One pound of yarn |
| Cotton | 1 | 840 yards | One pound of yarn |
| Linen | 1 | 300 yards | One pound of yarn |

**Yarn size:** Yarn size is the equivalent of yarn count, yarn fineness or yarn density. It is a number that is a multiple of a standard length in one pound of yarn. The standard length depends on the type of fiber. In all cases, the larger the size number, then the

**Yarn structure:** The ply of yarn is specified along with its size. A slash separates the yarn size and the number of singles in the yarn. Once again, the convention varies depending on the fiber.

39

For woolen and worsted, the number of singles precedes the size: (number of singles)/(size). For example, worsted 2/20 means the yarn is composed of two singles each of size 20. The size of the plied yarn is the singles size divided by the number of singles or 10, in this example.

For cotton and linen, the size precedes the number of singles: (size)/ (number of singles). For example, cotton 30/2 means the yarn is composed of two singles, each of size 30. The size of the plied yarn is the singles size divided by the number of singles or 15, in this case.

The extent of twisting may be indicated by turns per inch (tpi) or degrees of twist angle. Twist angles are described as follows:

Soft spun—5°
Medium twist—20°
Hard spun—30° to 45°

The *direction* of yarn twist or spin is discussed in Chapter 2.

**Trade designations:** In purchasing yarns, you are likely to come across these terms:
*Crewel yarn*—a thin, lightweight, 2 ply medium-twist yarn
*Persian yarn*—a soft-spun, 3 ply yarn made up of medium-twist 2 ply yarns
*Tapestry yarn*—a 4 ply, hard-spun yarn

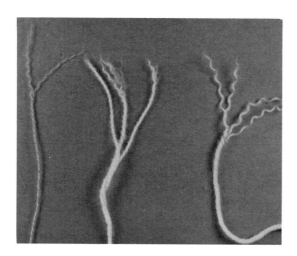

Figure 4-12. From left to right, crewel yarn, Persian yarn and tapestry yarn.

**Yarn suppliers**

Like oriental rug weaving, oriental rug repair is labor intensive. The cost of materials is minor compared to the cost of labor. Since there's no point in investing a lot of labor in inferior materials, it's wise to use the best yarns available for your repairs.

These addresses of yarn suppliers were correct at the time of publication. Note that product lines carried by suppliers may change.

**Pile yarns:** In general, the best yarn for pile repairs is Appleton yarn. These yarns are offered in about 380 colors and color cards are available at a modest cost. The colors tend to be the darker shades most often found in rugs. Appleton yarns are produced as crewel yarn and as tapestry yarn. Crewel yarn is preferable for repairs because it is slightly glossier and it can be unplied more easily than tapestry yarn. Appleton yarns are available from:

American Crewel and Canvas Studio
12 Edsel Avenue
P.O. Box 397
Nanuet, New York, 10954
Phone: 914 623-1691

Maury Bynum Oriental Rugs
Suite 100
500 N. Michigan Avenue
Chicago, Illinois 60611
Phone: 312 337-5555

Needle Arts, Inc.
2211 Monroe Street
Dearborn, Michigan 48124
Phone: 313 278-6266

Paternayan yarns are produced in about 350 colors. Color cards are available. Paternayan yarns can be purchased from:

Paternayan Bros., Inc.
312 East 95th Street
New York, New York 10028
Phone: 212 876-9600

**Natural (undyed) wool yarn:**

> John Wilde & Bro., Inc.
> 3705 Main Street
> Philadelphia, Pa. 19127

> Glimakra Looms and
>     Yarns, Inc.
> P.O. Box 16157
> Rocky River, OH 44116

**Goat hair yarn:**

> Greentree Ranch Wools
> 163 N. Carter Lake Road
> Loveland, Colorado 80537
> Phone: 303 667-6183

**Yak hair and camel hair:**

> The Fiber Studio
> Foster Hill Road
> Henniker, New Hampshire 03242
> Phone: 603 428-7830

**Alpaca and llama wool:**

> Scott's Woolen Mill
> Heck Street and Elmdale Road
> Uxbridge, Massachusetts 01569
> Phone: 617 278-6060

**Linen:**

> Novitex
> P.O. Box 440
> Pawtucket, Rhode Island 02862

> Frederick J. Fawcett, Inc.
> 129 South St.
> Boston, Massachusetts 02111
> Phone: 617 542-2370

1. Judd and Kelly, *Color-Universal Language and Dictionary of Names,* National Bureau of Standards, 1976, p.2,3.

2. V. Birrell, *The Textile Arts,* Harper and Brothers, 1959, p.41,42.

# Chapter 5

# Reknotting

Older literature about oriental rugs refers to the symmetric knot as the Turkish or Ghiordes knot and the asymmetric knot as the Persian or Senneh knot. These geographical references are misleading since both the symmetric and asymmetric knots are used throughout the middle east. Curiously, most rugs woven in Senneh (now Sanandaj, Iran) use the Turkish knot.[1]

Ghiordes is a rug-making town in Anatolia after which the knot is named. Ghiordes is not a reference to the Gordian knot, an impossibly complicated knot named for its inventor, Gordius, king of Phrygia.[2]

Since the knot that Alexander cut has never been found in a rug, it's beyond the scope of this chapter.

**Relative difficulty of reknotting**

Generally, three factors contribute to the difficulty of reknotting. These are knot density, warp offset and type of knot.

- Reknotting difficulty increases as knot density increases. At higher knot densities (above 100 per square inch), needle movements must be more exact. It may also be necessary to work from both font and back of the rug rather than from the front only. At very high knot densities, a magnifying visor or large magnifying glass on a gooseneck base will be needed.

- As warp offset increases, so does the difficulty of reknotting. Where warps lie on top of each other reknotting will proceed very slowly.

- The symmetric knot is easier initially to tie than the asymmetric knot. With the symmetric knot, needle movements are in the same direction while needle direction must be reversed in tying each asymmetric knot.

## Condition of the foundation

The rug should be clean and so arranged that one has access to both sides. The warp must be complete and sound. Broken warp must be restored before reknotting. Damaged or missing weft can be restored row by row as knotting proceeds. If there are signs of painting, the area should be tested for color fastness. Bleeding colors may be washed out. Do not remove worn knots until you are ready to replace them.

## Analyze existing knots and pile

It's important to take a close look at the knots and pile of the rug so you can copy the size, tightness and density of existing knots. If there is right or left slope to the pile, you'll want to reproduce this feature by orienting the knots on the warps.

Note the knot density; the more knots per square inch, the slower reknotting will proceed. The vertical knot count is not necessarily the same as the horizontal knot count. The vertical knots per inch are often greater than the horizontal knots per inch. The vertical knot count is proportionally greater if pile yarn size is small in relation to warp spacing. Also, the vertical knot count is increased if knots are beaten down tightly with a comb when the rug is first knotted.

With the symmetric knot, pile can slope to the right or left depending on how the yarn was pulled when the knot was tightened. The pile also slopes depending on the degree of offset of the warps. When a warp is completely offset, it lies behind another warp. In this case, both tufts of pile emerge to the right or left of the upper warp, even though the knot is symmetrical. This produces marked slope in the pile. It's most difficult to reknot rugs where alternate warp are completely depressed, such as Bidjars.

With the asymmetric knot, pile slopes to the right or left depending on whether the knot is open to the right or left. Slope is also increased depending on the direction the yarn is pulled as the knot is tightened.

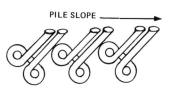

Figure 5-1. These symmetric knots are tied to warps offset about 45°. The pile slope tends to increase as warp offset increases.

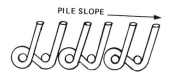

Figure 5-2. These are asymmetric knots open to the right. There is no warp offset. The pile slope direction results from the asymmetry of the knot.

Figure 5-3. These are asymmetric knots open to the left. There is no warp offset. The pile slope direction results from the asymmetry of the knot.

## Tools for reknotting

Only a few tools are needed for reknotting. These include:

- A selection of tapestry or yarn needles. These needles have large eyes to accept yarn and they have dull points. Dull pointed needles are best because they push warp and weft aside rather than piercing them.

- Small scissors. These should have slightly curved blades. They are used for trimming the pile and cutting yarn as knots are tied.

- Small shears. These are not essential. Used for cutting yarn after the knot is tied, they can be handled a little more quickly than regular scissors.

- Small, stiff-bristle fingernail brush. This is used to brush out the pile after knots are tied.

- Pile scissors. These are not essential, but are very helpful. Offset grips allow blades to remain parallel to the rug surface as pile is trimmed.

- Small leather mallet. This is used to hammer and spread new knots.

- Sharp pointed tweezers. These are needed in removing existing pile and worn knots.

- Sewing block. A piece of wood about five inches long and about two inches thick, square or cylindrical, will serve the purpose. The sewing block is used to lift the rug away from the table top or work surface so there is room for needle movement and it serves as a fulcrum for raising the warp with the needle. It also serves as an anvil when knots are spread by hammering.

- Small crochet hook. Knots can be tied using a fine crochet hook instead of a needle when the knot density is coarse. After you are familiar with the use of the needle, you may wish to experiment with a crochet hook.

Figure 5-4. A variety of tapestry needles. Note the dull points.

Figure 5-5. Scissors and spring shears. Top: scissors with short, curving blades. These are useful for cutting pile and yarn. Middle: pile scissors with an offset handle and a broad reference blade. Bottom: spring shears for rough-cutting pile and snipping yarn as knots are tied.

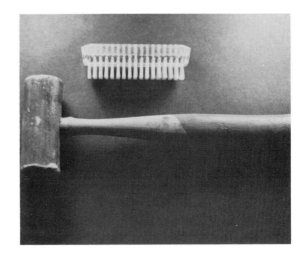

Figure 5-6. Fingernail brush for brushing pile and leather mallet for hammering new knots.

45

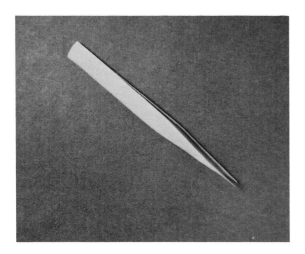

Figure 5-7. Sharp-pointed tweezers for removing old knots.

## Reknotting a rug—overview

The overall reknotting process includes these steps:

1. Removing worn knots
2. Tying new knots
3. Beating wefts and knots downward on the warps where necessary
4. Trimming the pile as each row is knotted
5. Brushing the pile
6. Spreading the knots by hammering
7. Brushing the pile again
8. Steam pressing
9. Touch-up trimming

These steps will be described in detail.

## Some reknotting guidelines

There are several guidelines that will help you reknot areas more efficiently, whether you are tying symmetric or asymmetric knots.

In an area to be reknotted, begin with the lowest row first. It's more difficult to tie knots under an overhanging pile. The pile must be pushed aside or pulled back to expose the warp for the needlework. Also, the pile of the upper knots tends to get trapped in the loops of the lower knots as they are pulled tight. Work from the bottom up, row by row, to cover an area with knots. If you are right-handed, it's easiest to work on rows from left to right.

Do not pull out old worn knots until you are ready to tie new ones on the same row. The old knots serve two purposes. They are reminders of the pattern and color scheme you must follow and they are place holders between the wefts. If you pull out two adjacent rows of knots before reknotting, three groups of wefts are exposed with nothing to separate them. With handling, these wefts move close to each other. Then, you have the task of identifying the wefts to be separated when you start tying knots. This will slow the reknotting process.

Figure 5-8. Sewing block to provide clearance and leverage for the needle.

Remove worn knots by working from the front of the rug. Use sharp pointed tweezers to loosen the knot loop—first one side, then the other. The yarn will then pull freely from the rug.

Several tapestry needles can be threaded with yarn of each color when there are frequent color changes in an area to be reknotted. With the needles already threaded, reknotting will move along more quickly.

Chapter 4 described yarn selection in detail, but a reminder is appropriate. Make sure you have the correct yarn size by tying some test knots and comparing them to the existing knots. If you are in doubt about the amount of yarn to use in your needle, use less.

Plied yarns should be unplied as far as practical for tying knots. The resulting singles in the needle should be kept fairly parallel as knots are tied. Keeping the singles parallel will fill the space more evenly and present a smoother and more consistent knot appearance from the back of the rug. As you tie knots, pull the yarn in the needle through your fingers to keep it straight and parallel.

Before reknotting, position the sewing block under the rug so that there is space for needle movement under the rug.

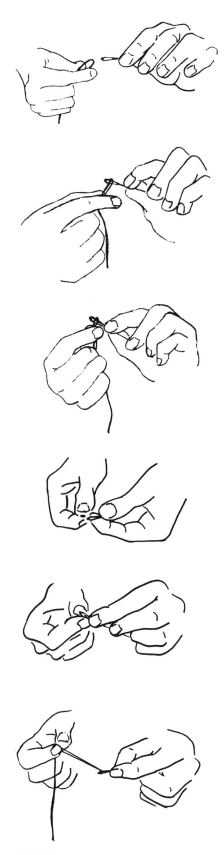

## Threading the needle

Use any method of threading the needle that works, but we recommend this one because it's quick and efficient.

1. Hold the needle horizontally with the eye sideways in the left hand. The edge of the eye is upwards.

2. Loop the yarn over the center of the eye.

3. Grasp the loop and the eye between the balls of the thumb and forefinger of the right hand.

4. Withdraw the needle.

Figure 5-9. Steps in threading the needle.

5. Hold the needle eye tightly in the cleft between the fingers above the loop of yarn. The eye of the needle is horizontal.

6. With a rolling motion, bringing the thumb upwards, force the loop through the eye of the needle.

With a little practice, you'll find this is an easy way to thread a needle.

## Tying the symmetric knot

These instructions assume the individual tying the knot is right handed.

1. Work from the front of the rug with the bottom of the rug downward.

2. Locate the two warps on which the knot will be tied. If tne wefts are close together where the knot will be tied, the wefts can be spread slightly by prying with the needle point.

3. With the tapestry needle threaded, insert the needle from right to left between the two warps so the point of the needle moves under the left warp and back to the front of the rug.

4. Pull the yarn under the left warp until there is about one half inch of yarn remaining between the warps.

5. Crossing both warps, insert the needle from the right under the right warp. The point of the needle should come up between the two warps.

6. Pull the needle from between the warps so the loop of yarn crosses, *above* both the half-inch tuft of yarn and the yarn attached to the needle.

7. Hold the half inch tuft of yarn with the left hand and draw the knot tight by pulling the yarn attached to the needle.

8. With scissors, clip the yarn attached to the needle so two half inch tufts remain at the knot, and the knot is complete.

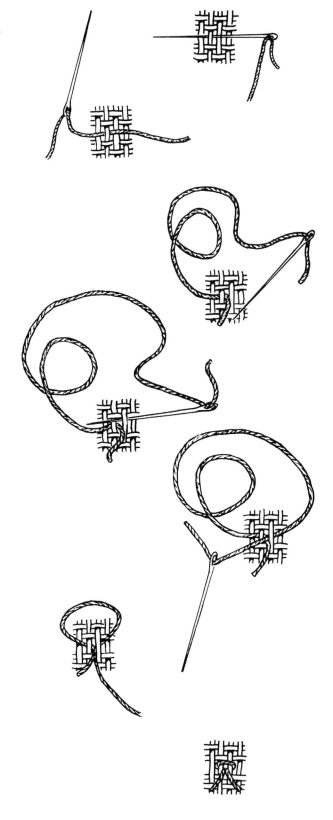

Figure 5-10. Tying the symmetric knot.

48

After you become very famliar with the symmetric knot, you can tie following knots in the same color on the same row without stopping to cut the yarn between each knot. A remaining loop of yarn connects each knot. This loop is cut as the new pile is trimmed to the final pile height. This method speeds knot tying of rows where there is one color.

## Speed in tying the symmetric knot

Your goal is knots consistent in quality with those in the rug, Speed will come naturally with practice. Knot size, density, warp offset, and number of color changes in a row all affect the rate of knot tying. For a rug with moderate knot density, say 50 knots (symmetric) per square inch with no warp offset or color changes, you can expect to tie about six knots per minute. This is somewhat slower than the rate at which rugs are originally knotted. With initial knotting, movement is not hampered by shoots of weft above the knot.

For coarsely woven rugs, you may find that you can pick up some speed by using a crochet hook instead of a needle.

Figure 5-12. Symmetric knot—yarn pulled under the warp.

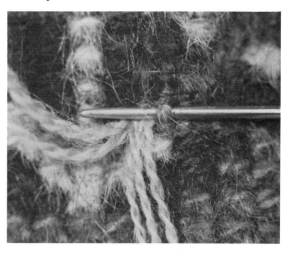

Figure 5-13. Symmetric knot—the needle under the second warp.

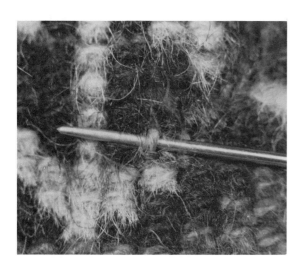

Figure 5-11. Symmetric knot—the needle under the first warp.
*Provenance:* Yastik
*Pile:* wool, symmetric knot, 49 knots per sq. in.
*Warp:* wool, 2-ply, "S" spun overall
*Weft:* wool, 3 to 6 shoots, "Z" spun singles

Figure 5-14. Symmetric knot—drawing yarn under the second warp.

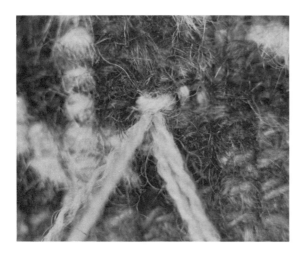

Figure 5-15. Symmetric knot—tightening the knot loop.

Figure 5-16. Symmetric knot before final trimming.

8. With scissors, clip the yarn attached to the needle so two half-inch tufts remain at the knot, and the knot is complete.

## Tying the asymmetric knot open to the left

1. Work from the front of the rug with the bottom of the rug downward.

2. Locate the two warps on which the knot will be tied. The knot loop will be formed on the right warp. If the wefts are close together where the knot will be tied, the wefts can be spread slightly by prying with the needle point.

3. With the tapestry needle threaded, insert the needle from left to right under the right-hand warp. The needle point should pass under the warp and return to the front of the rug.

4. Draw the yarn under the right-hand warp until one-half inch remains projecting between the two warps.

5. Bring the needle back over the right-hand warp and insert it from right to left between the warps directly above the projecting yarn end.

6. After passing under the left-hand warp, bring the needle point back to the surface of the rug.

7. By pulling the needle, draw the loop of yarn tight.

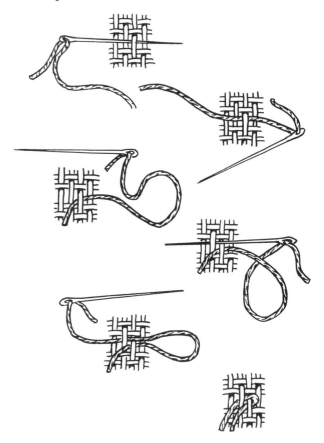

Figure 5-17. Tying the asymmetric knot open to the left.

## Tying the asymmetric knot open to the right

1. Work from the front of the rug with the bottom of the rug downward.

2. Locate the two warps on which the knot will be tied. The knot loop will be formed on the left warp. If the wefts are close together where the knot will be tied, the wefts can be spread slightly by prying with the needle point.

3. With the tapestry needle threaded, insert the needle from right to left under the left-hand warp. The needle point should pass under the warp and return to the front of the rug.

4. Draw the yarn under the left-hand warp until one-half inch remains projecting between the two warps.

5. Bring the needle back over the left-hand warp and insert it from left to right between the warps directly above the projecting yarn end.

6. After passing under the right-hand warp, bring the needle point back to the surface of the rug.

7. By pulling the needle, draw the loop of yarn tight.

8. With scissors, clip the yarn attached to the needle so two half inch tufts remain at the knot, and the knot is complete.

### Speed in tying the asymmetric knot

Speed will develop naturally with practice. Concentrate on tying knots consistent in quality with other knots in the rug. Warp offset, knot density and color changes will affect your speed in tying the asymmetric knot. Expect to tie about four to five asymmetric knots per minute.

Because the symmetric knot can be tied more rapidly, you may find old repairs consisting of symmetric knots tied in a rug woven with asymmetric knots. We do not recommend this practice. Use the knot appropriate for the rug.

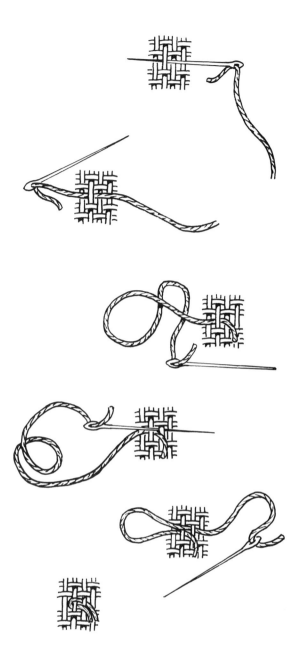

Figure 5-18. Tying the asymmetric knot open to the right.

### Problems in knot tying

You may find tufts of other knots trapped in new knots as they are drawn tight. These tufts must be pulled free of the new knot using either the needle point or tweezers. Do this as soon as you notice the pile is caught, otherwise the knots and pile will become tangled.

51

If a rug is pliable or loosely woven, the needle is not passed entirely through the rug. The point passes completely under the warp with the needle remaining on top of the rug. However, in a rug with a stiff foundation, a warp may break as it is raised due to the levering action of the needle. To prevent this from occuring when reknotting stiff or very tightly woven rugs, the needle must be passed entirely through the rug and point and needle must re-enter from the back of the rug .

Stiff or tightly woven large rugs with reknotting required in the center can be difficult to handle if the needle must be passed entirely through the rug. Reknotting will be speeded for such a rug if it is suspended and *two* repairers work on the rug, one on either side, passing the needle back and forth through the rug.

**Knot tightness and pile direction**

How tightly should you draw the knot? The warps should not be distorted and the knot should be the same size as the other knots in the rug. Inspect the completed knot from the back of the rug to see if it is similar to the others. If the new knot sinks into the warp and weft more than others, it's too tight.

Knots will rotate slightly on the warps towards the side drawn most tightly. If the right-hand pile is drawn more tightly, the pile will slope to the right. If both tufts are pulled sharply to the left or right as the knot loop is tightened, then the pile slope is further increased. One should try to duplicate the original knot tightness and pile slope. This is especially important where the finished pile will be cut back to expose knot loops on the front of the rug. In this case, pile slope is quite visible.

**Beating new knots downward on the warps**

Where new knots are tied singly surrounded by existing knots or in a row between two rows of existing knots, then there is no need to beat knots downward on the warps. However when a nunber of rows of new knots are tied and the foundation of the rug is loosely woven, each new row should be pressed downward on the warps towards the bottom of the rug.

Here is the procedure. The first and lowest row of the area to be reknotted is cleared of worn knots. The new knots are tied in this row and trimmed. Then, the adjacent upper row is cleared of worn knots. At this point, a comb or fork can be inserted above the wefts above the first row of new knots. Pressing downward with the comb or fork several times sets the first row of new knots firmly against the lower wefts and lower row of existing knots. This process is repeated for each row of new knots, except the top row which would be adjacent to a row of existing knots. If the warp spacing is fine or very narrow, tweezers or a needle point can be used to press wefts and knots downward.

As new rows of knots are beaten down, they should be straight, parallel and consistent with existing knot rows. If new knot rows are wavy or inconsistent with existing knot rows, then beating pressure is too little or too great, knots are too loose or too tight, or yarn size is incorrect.

**Trimming, brushing, hammering and pressing**

After each row of knots is tied, the pile should be rough trimmed, cutting any loops that link knots together. The pile is then brushed towards the bottom of the rug to untwist the fibers in the yarn.

For trimming the pile, you may use small sharp slightly curved scissors or special pile scissors. The broad lower blade of pile scissors rests on the pile to serve as a reference. The handle is offset so the blades remain parallel to the rug surface during cutting.

When pile wears, each tuft tends to adopt a slightly tapered brush shape. The tuft end is beveled from the upper to the lower surface in the direction of the pile. If new pile is clipped by moving the scissors parallel to wefts and cutting the tufts sharply, the new pile will not appear naturally worn. The appearance of wear is more closely copied if new pile is brushed towards the bottom of the rug and the scissors are held parallel to warps with the points towards the bottom of the rug during finish clipping.

Flattening and spreading of the knots occurs with normal usage in rugs. This same condition is achieved in new knots by hammering them. Hammering spreads the knot so it completely fills up the area between the wefts and between adjacent knots on the same row. Use a small leather mallet and a block of wood as anvil. A metal hammer or block might cut into the fibers during hammering. Place the area to be hammered, pile up, on the block and strike each portion of the knotted row two or three times.

The pile is brushed again before pressing to remove yarn and fiber cuttings and to position the pile. Brush the pile in the direction (sloping to right or left) you wish it to lie after pressing.

The newly knotted area is steam pressed using an iron hot enough to steam over a dampened thin pressing cloth. During pressing, the iron should be moved firmly in the direction you wish the pile to lie. Spreading the knot and steam pressing are essential steps in reknotting. They insure the yarn fibers settle into place and are "locked". Without these steps, the knot will loosen. When pressing is finished and the rug is dry, any required touch-up trimming completes the repair.

Trimming is a critical step because pile clipped too low must be reknotted. It's better to lower new pile height gradually rather than risk cutting it too low. Trim only one row at a time after the row of knots is tied and before the next row is begun.

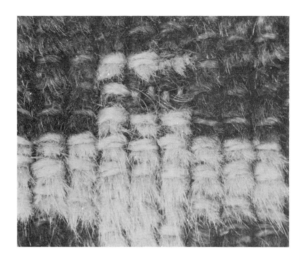

Figure 5-19. The front before reknotting.
*Provenance:* Yoruk
*Pile:* wool, symmetric knot, 48 knots per sq. in.
*Warp:* wool, 2-ply, "S" spun overall
*Weft:* wool, 3 to 6 shoots, "Z" spun singles

Figure 5-20. The same location on the back before reknotting.

Figure 5-21. A row cleared of old knots for reknotting. Note that work starts on the bottom row of the area to be reknotted.

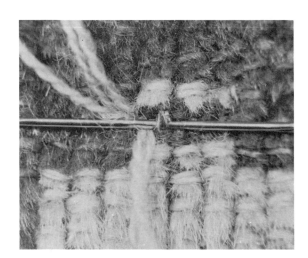

Figure 5-23. Yarn pulled under the first warp.

Figure 5-22. Passing the needle under the first warp to tie the first symmetric knot.

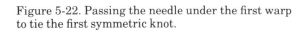

Figure 5-24. Passing the needle under the second warp.

Figure 5-25. Drawing down the first knot loop.

Figure 5-27. Starting the second knot.

Figure 5-26. The first symmetric knot.

Figure 5-28. The second knot is linked to the first by a loop of yarn that will be cut.

Figure 5-29. Passing the needle under the second warp of the second knot.

Figure 5-31. The first and lower row of symmetric knots with uncut yarn between them.

Figure 5-30. Two symmetric knots linked.

Figure 5-32. Rough cutting the first row of knots.

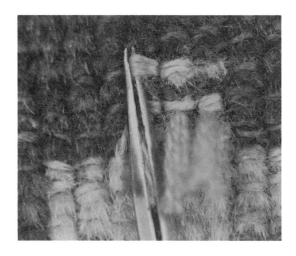

Figure 5-33. Removing a worn knot from the upper row.

Figure 5-35. The upper row cleared of old knots and ready for the new knots.

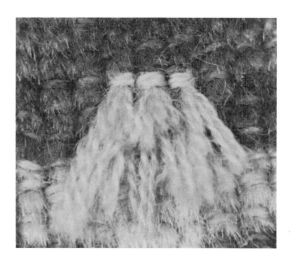

Figure 5-34. Spreading the wefts and pressing them downward against the first row of new knots.

Figure 5-36. The upper row of knots after rough cutting.

Figure 5-37. The reknotted area before the finishing steps.

Figure 5-39. Brushing the reknotted area.

Figure 5-38. Hammering the new knots to spread and lock them in place.

Figure 5-40. Final trimming of the new knots. Note the position of the scissors.

Figure 5-41. The back of the reknotted area.

Figure 5-42. The reknotted area after final trimming and pressing. The pile of the new knots was trimmed to match the surrounding area.

## Reknotting along selvages and ends

Selvage warps are structurally essential and these should be complete and sound before reknotting is done close to an edge. Finish binding of selvage should be done after any needed repair of wefts is completed. If wefts are restored as reknotting proceeds, then finish binding is done after edge knotting is completed. If both wefts and selvage are sound, then finish binding can be done before reknotting. See Chapter 7.

There are some Turkmen rugs that are made with asymmetric knots in the field with one or two columns of symmetric knots at the edges. Check for this possible knot variation when reknotting Turkmen rugs.

The bottom row of knots is prevented from sliding off the warps by a number of wefts, stitching or a killim end. This finish must be intact or knots will not stay in place. Complete bottom repairs to the end of the rug before tying knots in a row adjacent to the bottom end.

The end finish at the top of the rug should, of course, be repaired if it's damaged. But the top row of knots can be tied as long as the warps are sound. The end finish can be repaired afterwards. See Chapter 8.

Figure 5-43. Wefts are complete. Edge knotting can be done after finish binding.
*Provenance:* Yastik
*Pile:* wool, symmetric knot, 49 knots per sq. in.
*Warp:* wool, 2-ply, "S" spun overall
*Weft:* wool, 3 to 6 shoots, "Z" spun singles

Figure 5-44. Wefts are incomplete. Edge knotting should be done before finish binding.
*Provenance:* Yastik
*Pile:* wool, symmetric knot, 99 knots per sq. in.
*Warp:* wool, 2-ply, "S" spun overall
*Weft:* wool, 2 shoots, "Z" spun singles

## Differences between new and old pile appearance

In trimming new knots, you will want to match the pile height of adjacent worn areas. Even though you succeed in matching pile height and pile slope, there may be differences between new and old pile in the rug. Wool used in older rugs is often coarser and glossier than wool commercially available as yarn. This difference in wool quality may be evident. In addition, very fine wool fibers that project from newly spun yarn have worn off of older knots and pile. This is another difference in surface finish that may be noticeable on very close examination.

If large areas of a rug are to be reknotted, it's a good idea to select a small area as a test. Reknot, hammer, brush, trim and steam press this area. Only with this test can you be certain that texture and color match are close enough to be acceptable.

1. C. Neff and C. Maggs, *Dictionary of Oriental Rugs*, Van Nostrand Reinhold, 1979, p.123

2. *Brewer's Dictionary of Phrase and Fable*, Harper and Row, 1970, p.478

# Chapter 6

# Repairing Warp and Weft

If a rug is to withstand wear, its foundation must be whole and sound. If a rug is to be displayed, its appearance will be more pleasing without holes or tears. But, there are different methods of repairing a hole or tear. What method is best?

In discussing rug damage, we mentioned the repair alternatives for holes and tears. These are darning, using a plug, reknotting a coarse fabric patch, and reconstructing warp and weft. Of these, the most durable and aesthetically pleasing is reconstructing warp and weft. Careful reconstruction of warp and weft, along with reknotting, produces the least evidence of repair from both front and back of the rug. Reconstruction is a repair method that adds to the value of a rug. The other methods are expedients that usually detract from the value of a rug. For these reasons, reconstruction of warp and weft is the repair method we recommend for holes and tears.

**Major steps in repairing holes and tears**

You will find it helpful to keep the major steps of hole repair in mind as we describe the detailed procedures. Here are the major steps:

1. Remove damaged warps, wefts and knots to find the full extent of damage and to prepare the sound foundation as anchorage for new warps and wefts.
2. Build a wooden frame and mount the repair area of the rug on the frame to keep the repair area flat and under symmetrical tension
3. Anchor new warps by weaving them into the sound portion of the foundation.
4. Anchor new wefts by weaving them into the sound portion of the foundation as reknotting proceeds.

## Tools and materials for reconstructing warp and weft

Just a few tools and materials are needed for reconstructing warp and weft in addition to those needed for reknotting. These include:

- Sharp-pointed needles. A variety of sizes useful for anchoring warp and weft.

- Alligator-nose pliers with serrated gripping surface. These are used for pulling the warp-threaded needle through knots when the needle binds.

- Beeswax. Used to stiffen and lubricate new warp yarn so it passes through knots easily.

- Pocket comb. One that can be cut or broken into shorter lengths so the piece can fit into the damaged area. Used to press down new wefts and knots.

- Pushpins with aluminum tops or carpet tacks. These are used to attach the rug to the frame.

- Hammer, saw and wood to build the frame.

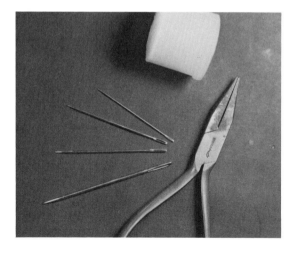

Figure 6-1. Materials and tools used for work on the foundation: beeswax, a selection of sharp pointed needles, alligator-nose pliers.

## Speed in reconstructing foundation

The basic time consumed in reconstructing foundation is weaving in new warps or rewarping. High knot density and warp offset increase the time needed for rewarping. Assuming a knot density of about 50 knots per square inch, no warp offset, and proper anchoring of the warp at *both* ends, new warps can be put in at the rate of about six per hour. The vertical dimension of the hole or new warp length does not add to the time for rewarping because it takes no more time to stretch a new warp across a large hole than a small hole.

Although rewefting tends to move more rapidly than rewarping, the time required for rewefting is more variable. The time required increases as there is an increase in:

1. Knot density
2. Horizontal length of the hole
3. Warp offset
4. Number of wefts between each row of knots

To estimate the total time for a hole repair, additional time allowances must be made for building the frame, mounting the rug on the frame, removing damaged material and reknotting. Locating the appropriate yarns may take a good deal of time, as well.

## Removing damaged material

The basic reason for removing damaged warp, weft and pile is that they are unreliable anchorage for new foundation. But, damaged material also interferes with interweaving new warp and weft. Damaged foundation includes torn or broken warp or weft extending into the hole. If such material does not provide structural support, it should be removed.

Areas of foundation embrittled by rot are removed before repairs are attempted. For rot damage, the full extent should be determined before removing *any* damaged material. If rot damage is extensive, it may be best to leave the rug as it is rather than attempt reconstruction. Corroded or stained material adjacent to the hole may be removed, as well. Material adjacent to a hole in the foundation is often loose or stretched out of shape because it lacked structural support. If the distortion appears permanent, such material should also be removed.

Figure 6-2. Repair of this hole would be faster if the darkened areas were removed to shorten the perimeter and eliminate overlapping anchorage for new warp and weft.

## Removing sound material

These are general guide lines for removing sound material. Detailed preparation of the hole edge is done after the repair area is mounted on a frame and will be described later.

There are good reasons for removing some sound foundation in addition to the damaged material.

A goal in repair is to make reconstruction as invisible as possible. Traces of reconstruction should be minimal. Assuming a good color match in the pile, traces of work on the foundation are most evident from the

back of the rug. The edges of the reconstructed area, where new foundation is anchored in old foundation, tend to reveal where work has been done. Therefore, if the length of the perimeter of the repaired area can be reduced, there will be less evidence of repair. Often, it's possible to reduce the length of the perimeter by removing irregularities in the shape of the hole.

It takes more time to reconstruct foundation at the edge of the hole than in the center of the hole. This is so because additional time is needed to anchor new warp and weft in reconstruction at the edge of the hole. Here again, shortening the perimeter by removing irregularities can save a little time in reconstruction. However, there's a trade off, shortening hole perimeter, where this is possible, increases hole area.

When holes are close to each other, it may be best to remove sound foundation between them. Anchorage areas should not overlap. New wefts are woven into sound foundation through about eight warps or four columns of knots. New warps are woven into sound foundation about four rows of knots. If knot density is about 64 per square inch, then there are eight knots per inch. If two holes, located horizontally next to each

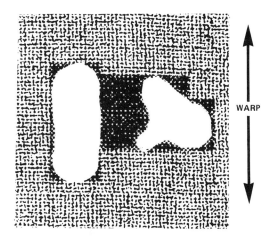

Figure 6-3. If holes are too close together weft-wise, as shown here, it may be best to remove the darkened areas to prevent overlapping weft anchorage.

other, are closer than one inch, the two anchorage areas (one-half inch around each hole) will overlap. In this situation, it's best to remove the sound foundation between the holes. If there were more knots per square inch, the anchorage areas would not overlap and the decision to remove the sound foundation might be different. Where two holes are located vertically close to each other with a narrow strip of sound material between them, then new warps can be run continuously across each hole and woven through the intervening sound material.

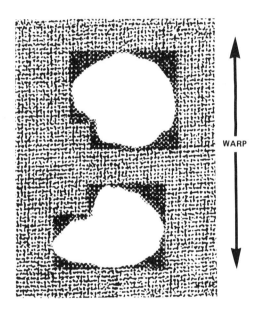

Figure 6-4. In this situation, new warps can be woven through the area separating the holes so that new warps are continuous.

Generally, in dealing with nearby holes, a minimum of about five columns or rows of knots should separate anchorage areas. Where this separation cannot be maintained, it's probably wiser to remove the sound foundation between the holes.

Of course, the concept of conservation should be weighed in deciding whether to remove sound material. Is the rug exceptionally rare or valuable? Will removal of sound material lower the rug's value? These are questions that should be answered before any rug is repaired.

## Making a frame

The purpose of mounting the damaged area on a frame is to keep the foundation under consistent and symmetrical tension as reconstruction proceeds. The frame keeps the repair area flat and permits work from both sides of the rug. The tension of new warps and wefts must be the same as warp and weft in the sound foundation. Otherwise, reconstruction will be irregular and produce wrinkles and puckers.

The frame size should allow a clear area between the edges of the hole and the frame of no less than three inches. A hole about two inches in diameter would require a frame of about eight inches on a side. If a hole or tear runs to the edge or ends of the rug, then the portion of the hole or tear nearest the center and sound portion of the rug is repaired first and the frame surrounds only that portion under repair. For a tear or cut, an elongated rectangular frame can be used.

The frame must be rigid. If it flexes or twists as work proceeds, then warps or wefts will be under uneven tension. The frame can be built from pieces of wood nailed together or it can be cut from a single piece of plywood.

For a nailed-up frame, pieces are a minimum of 3/4-inch thick. The frame is flat or flush on the side where the rug will be mounted. It's best if large nailed-up frames (a foot square or larger) are reinforced at the corners. Also, wider pieces of wood should be used. See the illustrated construction details. Frames can be cut from a single piece of 3/4-inch plywood using a sabre saw or key hole saw. Single-piece frames of plywood tend to be more sturdy.

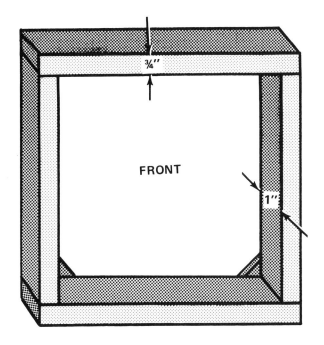

FRONT

¾"

1"

Figure 6-6. A frame made from a single pice of 3/4-inch plywood.

## Mounting the repair area on the frame

The hole or tear is centered over the frame and pushpins or carpet tacks are driven through the rug into the frame on all four sides. The pile is upwards and the pins or tacks are located at about one-inch intervals. Pushpins are preferrable to carpet tacks since they are less likely to cut into rug fibers. Pushpins with aluminum tops will not shatter when struck with a hammer while this can happen with plastic-topped pushpins. The pin or nail portion should be about one-half inch long.

Even and symmetrical tension over the repair area is very important. The repair area must be flat without sagging or tension wrinkles. After centering the hole or tear, attach the center of each side to the frame. Next, attach the corners. Then drive in additional pins or tacks, working from alternate sides. Place pins or tacks to increase tension evenly.

Broken warps and wefts must line-up across the hole or tear after the area is mounted on the frame. This is critical and may require some adjustment as the repair area is tacked to the frame. You can use a straight edge to be sure broken warps and wefts line-up properly.

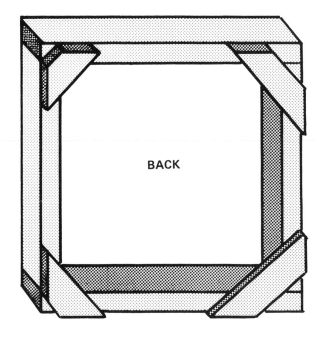

BACK

Figure 6-5. A nailed-up frame. This type of frame should be reinforced if it is larger than one foot on a side.

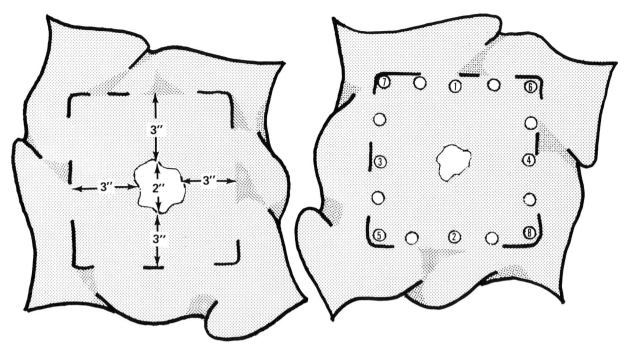

FRAME SIZE 8" x 8"

Figure 6-7. Note that a minimum 3-inch clearance must be left between the hole and the frame.

Figure 6-9. The numbers show the sequence to follow in tacking the rug to the frame.

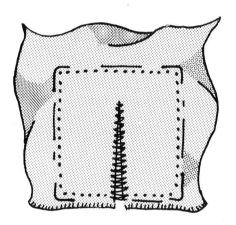

Figure 6-8. If holes or tears are large, they should be temporarily stitched when the rug is mounted on a frame.

Knots are removed from warp ends extending past the sound wefts into the hole. Top and bottom edges of the hole are wefts and not a row of knots.

Sound warps provide left and right edges of the hole. Tension of whole sound warps at the far edges of the hole should be the same as warp tension well into the sound area of the rug inside the frame. If warps at the hole edges are loose or stretched, they should be removed.

## Final preparation of hole or tear edges

Final preparation of the hole or tear edge is done after the repair area is mounted on the frame. Warps are cut back so they extend one-quarter to one-half inch into the hole beyond the sound wefts. These stub ends are grasped and pulled tight as new warps are interwoven beneath them. The sound wefts are top and bottom edges of the hole.

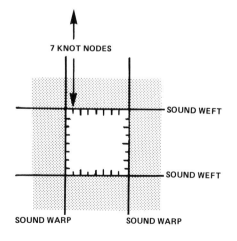

Figure 6-10. This is a diagram of a hole prepared for rewarping. The first new warp will be anchored under seven knot nodes next to a sound old warp.

66

## Rewarping

New warp yarn is matched in fiber type and color with existing warps just as pile yarn is matched. (See Selecting Yarn, Chapter 4). However, new warp yarn may be slightly smaller in size than existing warps . . . down to about two thirds original warp size. In no case should new warp yarn be larger in size than the original warp. Larger yarn would stretch knots excessively in the anchorage area.

A sharp pointed needle is used for rewarping rather than a tapestry needle. A tapestry needle won't penetrate the knot nodes. Select the needle with the smallest eye that will accept the new warp yarn.

Rewarping is done from the back of the rug. New warps are anchored by passing them under the knot node but above (from the back of the rug) the old warps. New warps piggeyback the old warps through the knot nodes and wefts.

After one end of the new warp is anchored under knots and wefts above the hole or tear, it is similarly anchored on the lower side of the hole. Without cutting the new warp, it is anchored under the knots and wefts along the adjacent old warp, brought across the hole again and anchored on the same side where it was first anchored. This process is continued, back and forth across the hole or tear until it is rewarped. Note that a single length of yarn is used to put in a number of new warps.

New warps are first anchored next to the sound warp at either edge of the hole. If you attempt to start rewarping from of the middle of the hole, you may misscount and thus missmatch the warps on the top and bottom of the hole. The warps will not be properly lined up. Always anchor your first new warp parallel with and next to a sound warp.

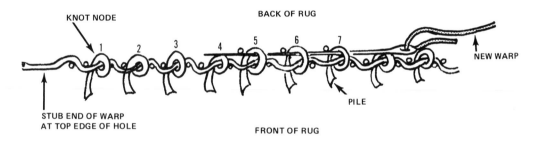

Figure 6-11. This is a section view of the rug. The length of the warp is shown. The wefts are seen in cross-section as small circles. The needle is in place as it would be in anchoring the first end of a new warp.

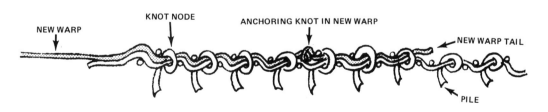

Figure 6-12. Here is the beginning end of the first new warp properly anchored. Note the knot tied in the new warp between the fourth and fifth knot nodes from the hole.

## Anchoring the end of the first new warp

Working from the back of the rug, here are the steps in anchoring the first new warp:

1. Lubricate the new warp yarn by pulling it across the beeswax. This will help the new warp move through knots more easily and help prevent new warp breakage.

2. Locate the incomplete warp next to a whole sound warp.

3. From the weft along the upper edge of the hole, count seven knots upwards along the warp to be restored.

4. Insert the needle point under the node of the seventh knot, but on top of the old warp. The needle points back along the old warp towards the hole.

5. Carefully guiding the point of the needle, pass it along on top of the old warp under knot nodes and through wefts. Be absolutely certain the new warp lies *on top* of the old warp and not to either side. Bring the needle to the surface after it passes under the third knot.

NOTE: The point of the needle should not penetrate the yarn of the wefts, but pass between wefts and above the old warp. The point of the needle should not penetrate the yarn of the knot node, but pass under the node and above the old warp. It may take several attempts to guide the needle point properly. Slow careful work produces the best results.

6. Draw the yarn through knot nodes and wefts until there is a one-inch yarn stub extending above the seventh knot.

7. Tie a square knot in the yarn attached to the needle close to the rug surface.

8. Reinsert the needle at the point where it emerged. Pass the needle along the old warp, through the wefts and four remaining knot nodes. The new warp must be *on top* of the old warp and not to one side.

NOTE: The needle may bind in the knots. In this case, you can back up the needle and try again or bring the needle to the surface and pull it out with the pliers. The needle is then reinserted at the point where it surfaced.

9. After passing along the top of the old warp, under knot nodes and through wefts, the needle and yarn are pulled into the hole or tear.

10. Pull the needle and yarn tight to press the square knot against the rug at the fourth knot node. Also, pull the stub end of the yarn above the seventh knot node. The new warp is locked in place with the square knot. The square knot is tied only at the two ends of the new warp and not at intermediate anchoring sites.

11. With the new warp firmly seated, the stub, end of the warp yarn above the seventh knot node can be clipped flush with the back of the rug. One end of the first warp is now anchored above the hole or tear.

## Needle binding and new warp breakage

One cannot avoid the problem of occasional needle binding in rewarping. It usually stems from one or more of these conditions:

- The needle is too large.
- The needle is penetrating weft yarn or knot yarn instead of passing along the top of the old warp between wefts and knots.
- The needle is penetrating old warp rather than passing above it.
- The knots or weave are quite tight and only a couple of knots and wefts should be picked up on the needle shaft before the needle point is brought to the surface.

Although pliers can be used to pull the needle through when it binds, too much force or the frequent use of force stretches the knots and distorts the weave. These dis-

68

tortions are permanent and will remrain visible in the anchorage area. If the needle binds constantly due to reasons other than needle movement or needle size, then pick up only a couple of knots at a time on the needle shaft.

If there is excessive friction when new warp yarn is pulled through knots, the yarn tends to break. Using beeswax on the new warp yarn will minimize this breakage. However, there will still be stress on the new warp yarn at the point where it passes through the eye of the needle. This is often the point of breakage. Breakage of the yarn in the eye of the needle can be reduced by slightly varying the point where the new warp yarn passes through the eye. Shift the location of the needle on the new warp yarn after it passes through a group of knots.

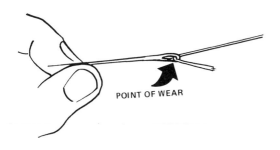

Figure 6-13. Yarn breakage at the needle can be reduced by shifting the needle on the warp yarn to avoid heavy wear at a single point.

### Anchoring the other end of the first new warp

One end of the first new warp is now anchored in the rug at the top edge of the hole. The other end is to be anchored over the opposite old warp.

When the needle is worked along an old warp towards the hole, friction will not move the old warp because it is *pulled* away from the sound portion of the rug where it is firmly interwoven. However, when a needle moves along an old warp away from the

hole and into the rug, friction *pushes* the loose end of the old warp into the rug. A stub end of the old warp about one-quarter to one-half inch long was left overhanging the weft at the edge of the hole. Distortions will occur unless this stub end of old warp is grasped and pulled with fingers or pliers in an opposite direction to the needle movement as the needle passes over it. This prevents the old warp from buckling or being pushed into the rug.

With this in mind, here are the steps in anchoring the other end of the new warp:

1. Grasp the stub of old warp and insert the needle under the weft above the old warp and under the first knot node.
2. Continue to move the needle along the top of the old warp and bring the point out after it has passed under four knot nodes.
3. Draw the new warp tight. The tension of the new warp across the hole should equal the tension of the adjacent old sound warp. Test the tension of both warps by pressing your finger first against one and then against the other. If the new warp is loose, pull on it to tighten it. If the new warp is too tight, pull on the new warp where it crosses the hole to loosen it.

### Anchoring the second new warp

Here are the steps in anchoring the second new warp:

1. Insert the needle under the adjacent knot node (on the next old warp) with needle pointing towards the hole. The new warp is not cut where it crosses over from the first old warp to the second old warp. We will refer to this crossover point as a turnaround because this is where the new warp reverses direction.
2. Pass the needle under the nodes and through the wefts and pull the yarn

tight when it emerges at the hole. This will cause the loop of yarn between the two old warps to sink into the back of the rug and virtually disappear.

3. Locate the opposing old warp on the top edge of the hole. Grasp the old warp stub and keep it taut as the needle is inserted under the weft or knot node and moved along the top of the old warp.

4. Pass the needle under only three knot nodes and bring the needle to the surface.

5. Compare the tension of the second new warp to the tension of old sound warps inside the frame. Tighten or loosen the second new warp so it equals the tension of other warps. The second new warp is now anchored.

## Staggering warp turnarounds

A turnaround is the point where new warp yarn crosses from a knot node on one old warp to the adjacent knot node on the next old warp. Usually, rewarping a hole requires that a number of new warps be anchored. If the turnarounds for new warps occur on the same row of knots, three knots from the hole for example, then a ridge will be formed along that row of knots at the new warp turnarounds. This ridge will outline the upper and lower edges of the anchorage area on the back of the rug.

To prevent this distortion in the weave, turnarounds are staggered. Each pair of new warps is anchored under three to five knots. By staggering the turnarounds at three, four and five knots, no more than two adjacent new warps will bulk up the knots to the same row.

In the rewarping example we have just described, the initial anchorage of the first new warp on the top edge of the hole was seven knots. The anchorage on the lower edge for the same new warp was four knots with a turnaround beginning a second new warp. This second new warp was anchored

under three knots on the upper edge of the hole. After the turnaround at the third knot on the upper edge, the third new warp will be anchored under five knots on the lower edge of the hole. Variation in turnarounds should continue until rewarping is completed.

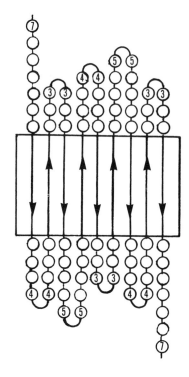

Figure 6-14. This is a schematic illustration of rewarping. Each circle represents a knot node. The number in the circle shows the number of knot nodes from the hole along the same warp. The arrows show the route of the new warp across the hole. Note that the new warp is anchored under seven knot nodes at the beginning and seven knot nodes at the end. Note, also, that new warp turnarounds are staggered.

## Anchoring the last new warp end

Rewarping continues back and forth across the hole or tear in the manner we have described until the last new warp end is to be anchored next to a sound old warp.

The last new warp end is passed under a minimum of three knot nodes. Then, a loose knot is tied in the new warp yarn close to the surface of the rug. The needle point is placed in a loop of the knot to keep the knot loose. The knot is worked down the new

70

warp yarn so it is placed as tightly as possible against the rug surface. The knot is tightened while the needle point holds it down against the rug. The remaining new warp yarn on the needle is passed under three more knot nodes, pulled tight and clipped flush with the rug surface. This completes rewarping the hole or tear. The rug remains mounted on the frame for re-wefting and reknotting.

**Tying new warps together**

The point where warp yarn in the needle will be used up should be anticipated. Additional new warp is tied where the new warp crosses the hole or tear because the tie point cannot be drawn under pile knots. A special weaver's knot is used to tie additional warp yarn to the newly anchored warp yarn. This knot is flat and permanent. The method of tying it is shown in the accompanying illustration. During reknotting, the warp stubs extending from the knot are pushed to the front of the rug where they are concealed by pile.

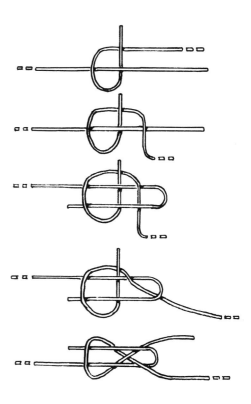

Figure 6-15. These are the steps in tying the weavers knot, used to tie warps together.

**Points to remember in rewarping**

The best rewarping is done by working slowly, carefully and following these guides:

1. Use the smallest needle size that will accept the new warp yarn.
1. Control the needle point so it does not penetrate knot yarn, weft yarn or old warp yarn.
3. Make sure new warp lies on top of old warp (from the back of the rug) and not to either side.
4. Check and adjust tension of each new warp.
5. Stagger turnarounds between 3 and 5 knots.

**Rewarping shortened runners or rugs**

When oriental rugs were generally considered as expendable floor coverings, rugs were sometimes cut to adjust the length to a particular location. This was done most frequently to runners. Shortened runners that have been cut and then stitched or even glued at the joint are now being presented for restoration of warp, weft and pile at the cut.

For this restoration, a frame is built somewhat wider than the full width of the rug. Except for the selvage, rewarping is done as described for holes or tears. The most critical step is positioning the cut portions of the rug on the frame. Here are some important points in mounting the two rug pieces:

71

- Study the design or pattern at the cut line and decide how much of the rug you will reconstruct. How does it match now? How should it match after reconstruction? Consider the amount of damaged material that must be removed to clean up the edges for rewarping. The extent of reconstruction can vary from a single row of knots to several inches. The rug pieces are mounted on the frame to allow the precise space needed for the number of rows of knots to be reconstructed.

- After mounting on the frame, the wefts in the two pieces must be exactly parallel. Warps should line up exactly along the two edges at the cut.

- Selvage warps are reconstructed before other rewarping. Selvage warps must also be in place before rewefting since wefts pass around the selvage before returning into the rug. See "Selvage and Edge Repairs", Chapter 7.

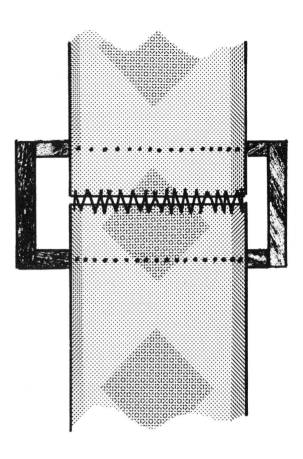

Figure 6-16. This diagram shows the way cut runners should be mounted for rewarping. The pieces are temporarily stitched together until they are rewarped.

## Preparation for the first new weft

There should be one or more complete wefts at the top and bottom edges of the hole. Crossing these wefts are new warps (from the back of the rug) and old warp stubs (from the front of the rug). Before the first row of new knots is put in, these old warp stubs are clipped back to the weft.

Old wefts are pressed or beaten down against the row of old knots before a new row of knots is tied. A needle point or comb segment can be used to do this.

Reknotting is begun from the bottom edge of the hole or tear and is completed row by row, working towards the top of the rug. With the old warp stubs clipped along the lower edge of the hole, the first row of knots is tied on the new warps against the existing lower weft.

## Rewefting

In addition to matching yarn color and size, new wefts reproduce these qualities of existing wefts:

- Number of wefts between rows of knots. This number may vary from row to row within the same rug.
- Shed. Whether the weft passes over or under a specific warp.
- Weft tension. Replacements for cable wefts must be drawn tightly; replacements for sinuous wefts bend around the warps.

Rewefting is done from the back of the rug using a sharp pointed needle. Rewefting proceeds upwards from the bottom edge of the hole as rows of knots are tied. The process of rewefting is similar to rewarping. The new weft is anchored through old warps and is woven through new warps back and forth cross the hole. The new weft is continuous. It passes under a knot node after each row of new knots is completed. The points where new weft reverses direction (turnarounds) are staggered.

## Anchoring the first new weft

A new weft is anchored by weaving each end through four to eight old warps. But, a special method is used to anchor the beginning and final ends of new weft. The starting end of the first new weft is anchored *parallel to and on top of an old warp.* Here are the steps:

1.  Locate the sixth old warp from the left or right side of the hole. On this old warp, locate the third knot node below the first weft to be replaced.
2.  With the sharp-pointed needle threaded with new weft, insert the point towards the top of the rug under this knot node.
3.  Pass the needle through wefts and under three knot nodes and bring it to the surface.
4.  Pull the new weft yarn through the wefts and knots so that only a one-half inch stub remains where the needle first went under a knot. You are now ready to weave your first new weft.

## Weaving new wefts

For the new weft, needle movements match the path of the old weft through the old warps. The first new weft will be woven through six old warps on either side of the hole. When the side of the hole is reached, the needle continues the alternation of the weft through the new warps above the row of new knots. On the opposite side of the hole, the needle movement continues next to the old weft and through the old warps

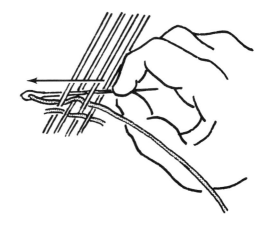

Figure 6-18. The needle is reversed so the eye moves forward in rewefting open warps.

There is a special technique in using the needle when it passes through new warps. Rather than point first, the eye of the needle is moved first through the *new* warps. This prevents the point from catching or penetrating new warps.

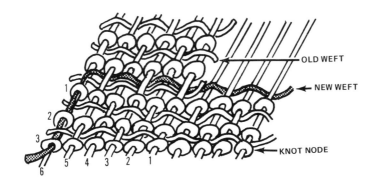

Figure 6-17. This diagram of the back of the rug shows the first new weft (dark yarn) properly anchored under three knot nodes and through six warps.

73

The new weft is pressed down or beaten against the row of knots using the needle point or a comb segment. Adjustment of new weft tension is usually needed at this point. Tension is increased by pulling on the new weft at the needle or loosened by pulling on the new weft with the needle point where it pass through the new warps.

In adjusting new weft tension, note warp offset and its affect on weft tension. Duplicate the tension (sinuous or cable) of old wefts.

Check the front of the rug to be sure no pile is trapped under the new weft. Free any trapped pile by raising it with the point of the needle. Readjust tension if necessary.

With the first new weft woven through six old warps on either side of the hole, the new weft reverses direction at the first turnaround. If the new weft is to return between the same row of knots, then it must pass around the last warp. If the new weft is to skip a row of knots in reversing direction, then the new weft passes under a knot node on top of a warp to begen the path in the opposite direction.

The turnaround of each new weft is staggered. Staggering turnarounds of new wefts is done to prevent a ridge from forming at the sides of the anchorage area. New wefts are anchored through a minimum of four old warps and up to eight old warps.

If a new weft should break or additional new weft is needed, additional new weft is overlapped four warps. Do not tie new wefts together.

A row of knots is tied after the appropriate number of wefts are woven through the warps. This process is repeated until the hole or tear is completely rewefted and reknotted.

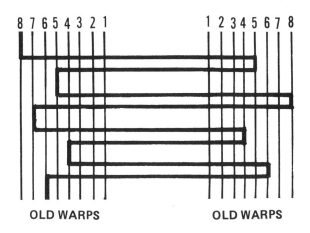

OLD WARPS      OLD WARPS

Figure 6-19. This schematic diagram shows old warps on either side of a hole as numbered vertical lines. Weft is shown as a heavy line with both ends anchored along old warps. Note that the weft turnarounds are staggered between four and eight old warps on either side of the hole.

The final end of the new weft is anchored on an old warp under three knots, as was the starting end. To finish rewefting, stub ends of the new weft are clipped flush with the back of the rug and the rug is removed from the frame.

### Copying the design when reknotting

Because of the size of a hole, details of the design to be reknotted may be lost. Usually, rug design is symmetrical. This allows you to copy design details from another area of the rug as guidance in reknotting a hole. It's easiest to copy a design, knot-for-knot, from the back or a rug. But, you are reknotting from the front of the rug. In the case of a large rug, checking the back repeatedly slows up the reknotting process. Work can be speeded by copying the design from the back, using colored pencils on graph paper. Each space represents a knot. The graph paper or "cartoon" is then used as your guide in reknotting from the front of the rug.

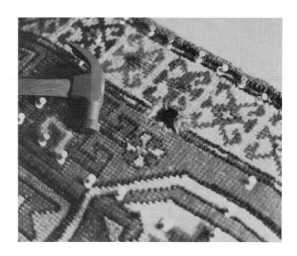

Figure 6-20. The next group of figures illustrates every stage in the repair of the hole shown here. This is the front of the rug.
*Provenance:* Karabaugh
*Pile:* wool, symmetric knot, 33 knots per sq. in.
*Warp:* wool, 2-ply, "S" spun overall
*Weft:* wool, 2 shoots, single, "S" spun

Figure 6-22. Here is the frame of plywood and pushpins.

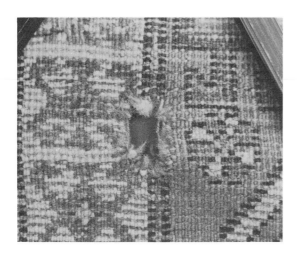

Figure 6-21. This is the hole from the back of the rug.

Figure 6-23. The rug is mounted on the frame.

Figure 6-24. The mounted rug from the back. Note the ample clearance around the hole.

Figure 6-26. The new warp is pulled under three knot nodes.

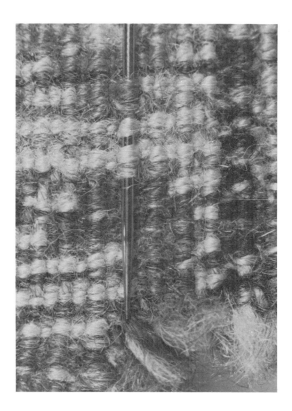

Figure 6-25. Anchoring the first warp end. The needle has picked up three knot nodes.

Figure 6-27. A knot has been tied in the new warp, the needle re-inserted, and the warp pulled through four additional knot nodes to properly anchor the new warp.

76

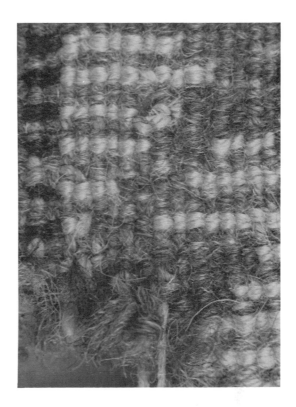

Figure 6-28. Here, the new warp has been pulled under four knot nodes on the opposite side of the hole.

Figure 6-30. The new warp loop at the turnaround disappears as the new warp is pulled tight.

Figure 6-29. This is the first turnaround of the new warp. Note the loop.

Figure 6-31. Here, the hole is partially rewarped.

Figure 6-32. Additional warp was needed. The knot was tied so it would be in the center of the hole.

Figure 6-34. This is the hole from the front of the rug after rewarping.

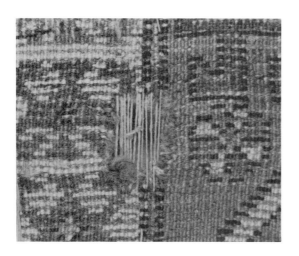

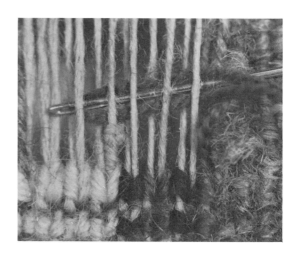

Figure 6-33. This is the hole from the back of the rug after rewarping.

Figure 6-35. Reknotting and rewefting have begun. New weft is inserted through free warps using the eye of the needle first.

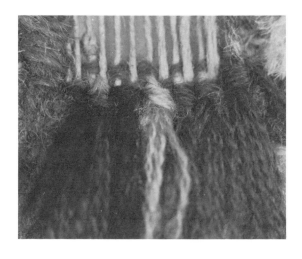

Figure 6-36. Uncut knot pile from the front of the rug.

Figure 6-38. The hole partially completed, from the back of the rug.

Figure 6-37. Reknotting and rewefting are partially completed as shown from the back of the rug.

Figure 6-39. The hole partially completed, from the front of the rug.

79

Figure 6-40. Reknotting completed with pile uncut.

Figure 6-42. The repaired area from the front of the rug.

## Appearance of reconstructed foundation

How do you know whether you've done a good job of reconstructing the foundation? The reconstructed area should blend in with the rest of the rug. Colors should match and the texture of the surface should be consistent throughout. Evidence of repair work on the back of the rug includes:

- Irregularities in the weave. These are avoided by duplicating as closely as possible the path and tension of existing and replaced warp and weft.
- Ridges where new warps or wefts begin or end. Staggering the anchorages for warp and weft prevent the formation of ridges.
- Loose stubs of yarn. These should be pushed to the front of the rug and clipped short enough to be concealed by pile, where this is possible.
- Warp knots. Draw knots tight, make them small, and push stub ends to the front of the rug.

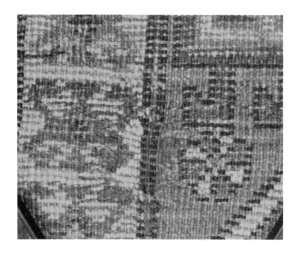

Figure 6-41. The back of the rug with the hole repaired. The distortion around the repair area is due to inadequate warp tension during repairs.

80

# Chapter 7

# Selvage and Edge Repairs

"Selvage" is derived from German for "self-edge". This suggests the edge of the fabric is a simple extension of the warp and weft or foundation. For some fabrics, this is true. But, for oriental rugs, the selvage has two special purposes. These are to take up warp space elsewhere occupied by knots and to strengthen the edge of the rug.

## Structural variations of selvage

You were briefly introduced to the structure of selvage in Chapter 2. There are many variations in that structure. To reconstruct a selvage, specific variations appropriate to the rug are studied and then copied. The following review of the most important features of selvage structure will help you do this.

There are five elements that can make up the selvage. These are:

1. Selvage warps. These are usually surrounded by wefts.
2. Wefts extending from the rug foundation and into or around the selvage warps. These are termed "ground wefts".
3. Wefts in the selvage that may or may not extend several warps into the rug foundation. These are termed "selvage wefts" and may be present only where there are multiple selvage warps.
4. Overcasting made up of yarn surrounding weft in the selvage and selvage warps, but not woven into the foundation.
5. Pile knots within the selvage tied at regular intervals between ground wefts or selvage wefts.

*Selvage warps.* Normally, there will be at least one selvage warp at either side, but there are many possible selvage warp arrangements. These include:

- A single selvage warp (same size as foundation warps or larger) around which the ground weft passes
- A bundle of selvage warps around which the ground weft passes
- Two or more single warps in the same plane
- Two or more bundles of warps in the same plane

Although selvage warps are usually the same size, type and color as foundation warps, this is not always the case. Variations in these features should be copied.

Where there are multiple warps in the same plane, these form a narrow strip of fabric at the edges of the rug. In this type of selvage, extra wefts are woven in the selvage at the ends of rows of knots in the foundation. The wefts in this fabric are ground wefts or both ground wefts and selvage wefts.

There are special cases where two or more rugs are woven side-by-side on the same loom. After weaving, the rugs are cut apart. In separating the rugs, the ground wefts are severed. There may be selvage warps around which ground wefts pass on only one side of the rug. Rarely, there will be an undamaged rug where ground wefts are cut on both sides of the rug. A false selvage is sewn to the rug by the maker at edges where ground wefts have been cut. These are low-quality rugs, usually of Pakistani, Indian or Chinese origin.

*Ground wefts.* Ground wefts are extensions from the foundation into the selvage. Where there are several selvage warps or warp bundles, the ground weft may be interwoven with all warps in the selvage, several warps in the selvage, or only a single warp or warp bundle in the selvage. Selvage warps that are not bound to the foundation by ground wefts are bound by selvage weft.

Figure 7-2. Selvage of ground weft. Here, ground weft is woven into six warps at the ends of knot rows. This produces a webbing or fabric along the edge of the rug. Also, see Figure 2-33.

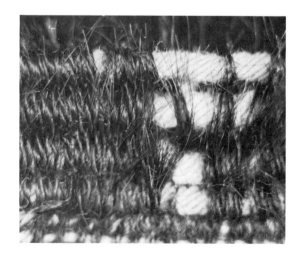

Figure 7-3. This is a selvage of four warps in the same plane with ground weft interwoven.
*Provenance:* Baluchi
*Pile:* wool, asymmetric knot open to the left, 56 knots per sq. in.
*Warp:* wool, 2-ply (except for edge warps), "S" spun overall
*Weft:* wool, 2 shoots, single, "Z" spun

Figure 7-1. Selvage of ground weft. Here, two warps are wrapped with ground weft at the ends of knot rows. Also, see Figure 2-30.

*Selvage wefts.* Selvage wefts are interwoven with selvage warps and hold them together. These wefts are not, strictly speaking, part of the rug foundation. Selvage wefts may, however, be interwoven with several foundation warps at intervals along the edge. Where this does not occur and there are multiple selvage warps, then the selvage wefts share at least one warp with ground wefts.

Selvage wefts are often differently colored than ground wefts. Where they are the same color, they can be distinguished from ground wefts only by very close examination.

Figure 7-4. Selvage with selvage weft. Note that ground weft does not extend all the way to the edge. Here, selvage wefts penetrate the foundation and share two warps with ground wefts.

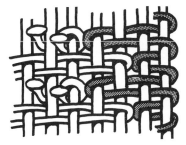

Figure 7-5. Here is an added selvage of two bundles. Overcasting of the warp bundles has been interwoven with the foundation as selvage wefts at intervals. This binds the added warps to the rug. Note that ground wefts (white) do not encircle the added selvage warps.
*Provenance:* Kurd
*Pile:* wool, symmetric knot, 49 knots per sq. in.
*Warp:* wool, 3-ply, "S" spun overall
*Weft:* cotton, 3 shoots, 2-ply, "S" spun overall

*Overcasting.* Overcasting is neither ground weft nor selvage weft, but yarn that surrounds these and the warps as selvage protection and, perhaps, as additional decoration. It may be very difficult to distinguish overcasting from selvage wefts or ground wefts when the same size, type and color of yarn is used for wefts and overcasting. It may be necessary to trace the paths of individual yarns to distinguish these elements.

Figure 7-6. Whip stitch overcasting. The overcasting covers wefts at the edge warps. Also, see Figure 2-31.

Figure 7-7. Whip stitch overcasting of two warp bundles.
*Provenance:* Salor
*Pile:* wool, asymmetric open to right, 152 knots per sq. in.
*Warp:* wool, 2-ply, "Z" spun overall
*Weft:* wool, 2 shoots, single, "Z" spun

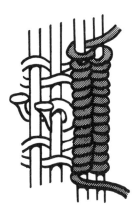

Figure 7-8. Figure eight stitch overcasting. The overcasting covers wefts at the edge warps. Also, see Figure 2-35.

For nomadic or village rugs, a variety of materials and stitch types are used in overcasting. Yoruk (Anatolian) rugs are sometimes overcast with a figure eight stitch that is tied at the waist. In some rugs, overcasting is combined with a braid or interlocking stitch. Baluchi rugs may be overcast with horse hair or goat hair. Overcasting may be in colored segments, checkered, or barber-pole stripes. Pompoms or cowrie shells can be attached to the selvage by overcasting. The most important structural feature of overcasting is the stitch.

Note these overcasting stitch characteristics to be copied in repair overcasting:

- Stitch type. Basically, this depends on the number of warps or warp bundles in the selvage. Where there is only one warp or warp bundle, then a whip stitch is used. Where there are two or more warps or warp bundles, then some form of the figure eight stitch is normally used.
- Stitch spacing and tightness. Stitches should be neat and regular, imitating the spacing and tightness of original overcasting. Where there are several warps or warp bundles, avoid drawing the figure eight stitch too tightly since this may cause the selvage to curl.

- Stitch angle. When a whip stitch is used on a single warp bundle, the stitch can cross the selvage warps exactly (parallel to the wefts), or it can be angled. Check this feature in the original overcasting.

Figure 7-9. A figure eight stitch overcasting over two warp bundles. Each warp bundle contains two warps. Selvage wefts penetrate the foundation after each row of knots. Ground wefts encircle only the first warp of the first warp bundle.
*Provenance:* Karabaugh
*Pile:* wool, symmetric knot, 56 knots per sq. in.
*Warp:* cotton, 5-ply, "S" spun overall
*Weft:* cotton, 2 shoots, 3-ply, "S" spun overall

Figure 7-10. Overcasting with figure eight stitch tied at the waist.
*Provenance:* Yoruk
*Pile:* wool, symmetric knot, 72 knots per sq. in.
*Warp:* wool, 2-ply, "S" spun overall
*Weft:* wool, 2 to 4 shoots, single, "Z" spun

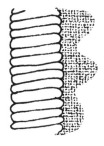

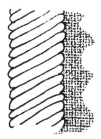

Figure 7-11. Variation in overcasting stitch angle. The original stitch angle should be copied.

*Selvage pile knots.* Some pile knots may be tied on selvage warps. These are tied between selvage wefts or ground wefts. Usually, selvage pile knots are not tied at every row of knots but skip rows of knots at regular intervals. Where selvage weft is differently colored than ground weft, the alternation of pile knots with several selvage wefts is a distinctive ornamental feature.

*Edge knot variation.* Although they are not part of the selvage, there may be variation of pile knot types at the edges of the rug, especially Turkmen rugs. Several columns of symmetric knots may be tied to edge warps while the field is tied with asymmetric knots. Keep this possibility in mind if you have edge repairs to do on Turkmen rugs.

## Overcasting the selvage

Selvage overcasting is the repair requested most frequently. Selvage is particularly subject to wear since it presents a less resil-

ient surface to traffic. Overcasting is valuable because it protects edge warps and wefts from wearing through and parting.

Usually it's best to copy the yarn type and color in the original overcasting. However, this is not always possible. Previous repair overcasting may not be compatible with the rug and there may be no traces of the original overcasting yarn. In this situation, select a yarn type, size and color used in the orignal overcasting of rugs of similar origin and age.

Before you begin any overcasting, be sure that selvage warps and wefts are in good condition. These cannot be satisfactorily repaired after the damaged area is overcast. Remove any loosened or broken original overcasting. Use a tapestry needle for overcasting. The stitch should match that of the original overcasting.

When overcasting, the edge of the rug is mounted on a frame or it can be mounted on the edge of a long board. The rug edge is held taut, no wrinkles or sags. If a frame is used, a frame one foot wide and one yard long is sufficient. The overcasting is done in sections. When one three-foot section is done, an adjacent section of the rug is mounted and overcast.

Figure 7-12. Selvage pile knots. The pile knots in the selvage are worn. They alternate with overcasting.
*Provenance:* Karabaugh
*Pile:* wool, symmetric knot, 33 knots per sq. in.
*Warp:* wool, 2-ply, "S" spun overall
*Weft:* wool, 2 shoots, single, "S" spun

Overcasting yarn is anchored at the ends by inserting the loose end under the overcasting and clipping the stub end. When yarn in the needle runs out during overcasting, several stitches are overlapped to conceal the loose end and begin a new portion of the selvage.

Although overcasting is a simple operation, it is time consuming. Depending on yarn thickness, stitch spacing and stitch type, overcasting can take from five to fifteen minutes an inch.

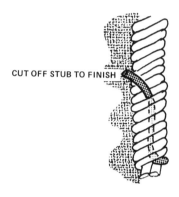

Figure 7-13. Anchoring the overcasting yarn end under the overcasting. The exposed yarn stub is cut off.

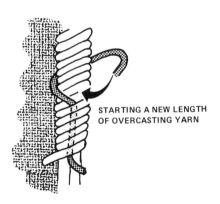

Figure 7-14. Overlapping overcasting yarn to begin a new section of overcasting.

Why not use machine overcasting? This would seem to be a reasonable alternative for inexpensive oriental rugs. There are some problems with this approach. Existing selvage must be cut off as preparation for machine overcasting. This significantly lowers the value of a rug. And then, machine overcasting appears to be just that, machine work. Machine work in combination with hand craftsmanship is discordant. To preserve the original character of an oriental rug, repairs by hand, including overcasting, are far preferable to machine work.

### Time required for selvage rewarping and rewefting

You are now familiar with the major structural variations of selvages. Complicating structural variations increase the time needed for repair. A high knot density requires more warps and wefts to the inch and this also increases selvage repair time.

Subject to these factors, here are approximate rates for rewarping and rewefting selvage. Assume a knot density of about forty knots per square inch. Rewarping and rewefting of ground weft only requires about one hour for two inches of selvage. If the ground weft is in good condition and only selvage weft is reconstructed then rewarping and selvage rewefting requires about one hour for five inches of selvage.

### Preparing damaged selvage for repair

To prepare the damaged selvage for reconstruction, loose and broken overcasting is removed to expose the damaged area. Loose ends of old overcasting are anchored by threading them in a needle or using a crochet hook to bring them back under the sound or tightly wrapped portion of the overcasting.

Any part of the damaged selvage that can contribute some structural support is saved until replacement warp and weft are about to be anchored in place. This is done because the damaged selvage is supported on only three sides during reconstruction. The unsupported selvage tends to stretch out of shape when placed under tension. To minimize this distortion, even loose warps are left in place. However, parted selvage warps are cut back to sound material. About one-half inch of old warp stub is left so that the old warp can be pulled taut as a needle is passed over it in rewarping.

Broken weft is left in place. Loose ends are removed two or three rows at a time and the stubs pushed to the front of the rug as rewefting proceeds. Leaving the loose weft in place until replacement weft is about to be anchored minimizes continued unraveling of the weft and loosening of warps and adjacent pile knots.

There's another reason for not removing all the damaged warp and weft in the selvage. You may get discouraged when you see the full extent of material to be recon-structed. If you *must* interrupt repair work on a rug, the remaining damaged material appears more natural than a surgically precise hole in the selvage.

## Basic steps in reconstructing a portion of selvage

In this description of selvage reconstruction, we'll assume that the warps next to the selvage are whole and sound. These are the basic steps:

1. Remove any loose and broken overcasting.
2. Cut back parted selvage warps to within one-half inch of sound selvage.
3. Construct a frame six inches longer than the damaged portion of the selvage.
4. Mount the damaged portion of selvage on the frame.
5. Rewarp the selvage.
6. Reweft the selvage.
7. Overcast the selvage if appropriate.

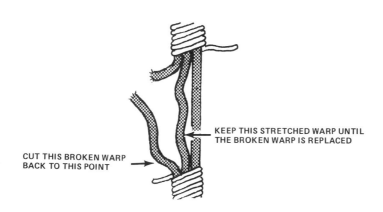

KEEP THIS STRETCHED WARP UNTIL THE BROKEN WARP IS REPLACED

CUT THIS BROKEN WARP BACK TO THIS POINT

Figure 7-15. Treatment of old stretched or broken warps in the selvage.

## Building a frame for selvage repair

Selvage and edge warps are kept under even tension during reconstruction so that wrinkles and distortions will not be woven into the repaired area. A frame is built to hold the repair area flat and taut during work. This frame is at least six inches longer than the damaged area at the selvage and three inches wider than the damaged area at its widest point. The frame can be an elongated rectangle and pieced together as described in Chapter 6 or it can be made of three pieces of wood; a board with projecting pieces nailed to either end.

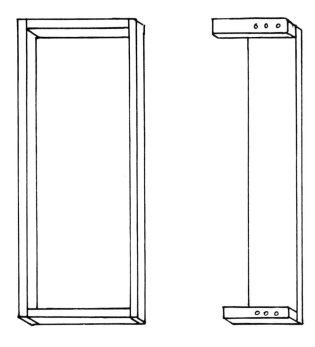

Figure 7-16. A rectangular frame and a board frame used in overcasting and selvage repairs.

## Mounting the damaged portion of selvage on the frame

Pushpins or carpet tacks are used to attach the rug to the frame. These should penetrate the sound selvage and sound portion of the rug. A two-inch width of selvage and rug is attached to the frame with about six pushpins or tacks at each end of the repair area. The pushpins or tacks are staggered.

The repair area is centered in the open portion of the C-shaped frame or inside a rectangular frame. If a rectanguular frame is used, one to two inches of open space is left between the damaged selvage and the parallel edge of the frame.

In mounting the rug, adjust the tension so that it is even and there are no tension wrinkles in the repair area. Where selvage warps have parted, do not stretch the repair area so tightly that distortion is apparent. The tension at the edge of the selvage is a matter of judgment and "feel". Too much tension will prevent the wefts from remaining parallel and stretch the area under repair. This would produce a wrinkle in the finished edge. Insufficient tension will make the repair area shorter than the original and produce a pucker in the finished edge.

## Anchoring new selvage warps

The procedure for rewarping selvage is similar to the procedure for rewarping foundation. New warp yarn is matched with the existing selvage warp yarn in color, size and type. New warp yarn is drawn over beeswax so it pulls through weft more easily and is less likely to break. A sharp pointed needle is used for rewarping. The size of the needle eye should be no larger than necessary to accept the new warp yarn. Selvage rewarping is done from the back of the rug. Loose or frayed old warps are left in place until new warps are anchored along the same path.

Identify a specific selvage warp to be replaced and then follow this procedure:

1. Locate the eigth sound weft (either selvage weft or ground weft) above the damaged area on the old warp to be replaced. Note that four wefts will pass over the old warp and four wefts will pass under it.

2. Insert the needle, pointed towards the damaged area, under the fourth weft passing over the old warp.

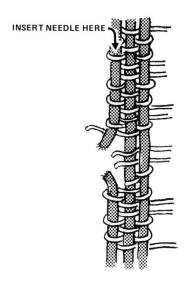

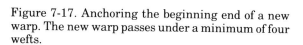

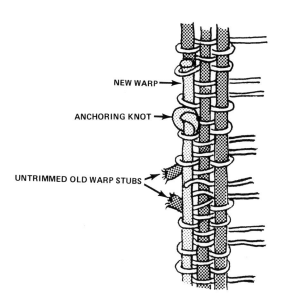

Figure 7-17. Anchoring the beginning end of a new warp. The new warp passes under a minimum of four wefts.

Figure 7-18. Anchored end of a new warp. A knot is tied after the new warp passes under two wefts to prevent slippage.

3. Bring the needle to the surface after it passes under two wefts. In so far as possible, the new warp should lie on top (from the back of the rug) of the old warp and not to either side.

4. Pull the yarn through until there is only a one-inch stub remaining above the fourth weft. Needle binding should not be a problem because wefts are normally looser than pile knots.

5. Tie a knot in the new warp close to the selvage. Re-insert the needle where it came to the surface, pointed towards the damaged area.

6. Bring the needle out from under the last sound weft above the damaged area and draw the yarn tight. This will seat the knot against the weft below it.

7. Pull on the new warp stub protruding from above the fourth weft crossing over the new warp to tighten the warp. Then, clip the stub flush with the selvage. You have anchored the upper end of the first new selvage warp.

NOTE: If the selvage warps are single warps in the same plane and several warps are missing, then you must be careful in bridging the damaged area with the new warp. The warps must line up across the damaged area. If several old warps are broken in the same bundle of warps, then warps need not be matched exactly within the same bundle.

8. Grasp the stub end of the matching old warp on the lower side of the damaged area. Pull it tight as the needle is passed over it and beneath crossing wefts.

9. The needle is passed under four crossing wefts. Pull the new warp yarn tight and compare the tension with that of adjacent sound warps. Adjust the tension of the new warp to match the tension of adjacent sound warps.

10. This completes the first new selvage warp. If this is the only warp to be replaced, then the new warp end is anchored in the same manner as new foundation warps (basically reversing the anchoring procedure of the initial new warp end).

NOTE: To replace broken warps *within* warp bundles, each replacement warp is anchored with a knot at both ends. There are *no* turnarounds. However, the knotted ends are staggered between two and four crossover wefts. If the selvage consists of single warps in the same plane, then new warp turnarounds are used.

11. For steps 11 through 14, assume that the selvage has single warps in the same plane with several adjacent broken warps. In this situation, warps are replaced in the order working from the warp closest to the field to the warp closest to the edge. We have anchored the first new warp and have reached a turnaround. The direction of the new warp is reversed by inserting the needle, pointed towards the damaged area, under the fourth crossover weft on the adjacent broken warp.

12. The needle is passed under the three remaining crossover wefts and out into the damaged area. When the yarn is drawn tight, the loop between the two old warps will sink into the selvage.

13. The new warp is carried across the damaged area and inserted under the opposing matching old warp while pulling on the old warp stub.

This time, the needle is inserted under only three crossover wefts to stagger the anchorage and turnaround points above the damaged area.

14. New warps are woven across the damaged area in this manner until all damaged and loose warps are replaced. Turnarounds are staggered. The final end of the new warp is anchored in the usual manner with a knot.

15. After damaged and loose warps are replaced, the old warps and warp stubs are cut away. This is done for warps in bundles and where there are single warps in the same plane. Damaged and loose warps and warp stubs are cut back to the sound weft crossing over them. This completes rewarping the damaged selvage.

**Rewefting a portion of selvage**

New weft yarn is matched with existing weft in color, size and type. Rewefting proceeds from the bottom of the damaged area upwards and any pile knots in the selvage are replaced as wefts are rewoven. A sharp pointed needle is used for rewefting. The point of the needle is used first when new weft is woven through sound material. The eye of the needle is used first when new weft is woven through areas where old weft has been removed or where old weft is loose.

In removing damaged weft, only two or three wefts are cut back at a time. This minimizes loosening of warps and adjacent pile knots. Stub ends of cut wefts are pushed to the front of the rug if they are in the foundation and to the back of the rug if they are in the selvage. This placement of stub ends should be done immediately after wefts are trimmed and before any rewefting is begun. The flat side of the needle at the eye can be used to push old weft stubs to the front of the rug.

Use the new weft anchoring procedure described in Chapter 6. In anchoring new ground wefts, they should overlap existing sound ground wefts through about six foundation warps next to the selvage warps. New weft passes through the same shed as the original weft. To cross a row of pile knots with new ground weft, the needle is passed under a knot node before returning the weft towards the selvage. Be sure to stagger these turnarounds. Match new weft tension with existing weft tension.

As each new weft is woven through the warps, it is beaten down. Use a segment of a comb for this purpose. There are three basic ways wefts are used in the selvage:

1. There is a single selvage warp or warp bundle. In this case, all wefts in the selvege are ground wefts. The selvage warp may or may not have extra ground weft wrapped around it at the ends of rows of pile knots. Copy this feature if present.

2. There are multiple selvage warps or warp bundles with only ground weft. The new ground weft is interwoven through the multiple selvage warps or warp bundles. Several shoots of weft that do not penetrate the foundation are probably located at the ends of knot rows. Look for this feature and copy it if it occurs.

3. There are multiple selvage warps or warp bundles with both ground weft and selvage weft interwoven. Carefully distinguish ground weft from selvage weft and identify the warps shared by both selvage wefts and ground wefts. Thread one needle with selvage weft yarn and another with ground weft yarn. The two types of wefts are woven on the appropriate warps, with both being completed at about the same rate.

After rewefting is completed, the selvage is overcast if required. The repaired area can then be removed from the frame.

Figure 7-19. The selvage area to be restored is mounted on the frame. Damaged warp and weft is being removed. Figures 7-19 through 7-32 show the same rug.
*Provenance:* Yastik
*Pile:* wool, symmetric knot, 49 knots per sq. in.
*Warp:* wool, 2-ply, "S" spun overall
*Weft:* wool, 3 to 6 shoots, "Z" spun overall

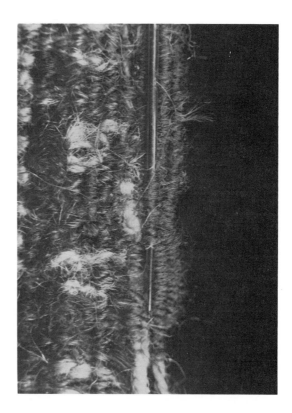

Figure 7-20. Anchoring a new warp. This is the back of the rug. Note how the needle lies on top of the existing warp.

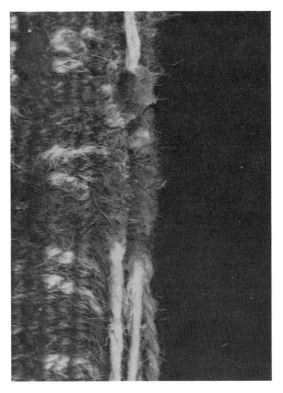

Figure 7-21. The new warp has been anchored under existing wefts. Excessive wax on the new warp has caked on the existing wefts. This wax can be cleaned off with naptha or cleaning fluid after repairs are completed.

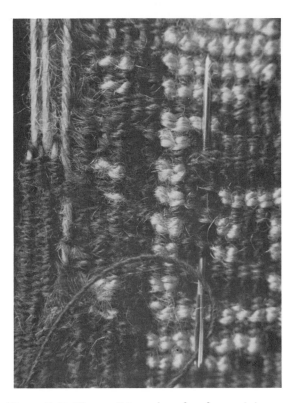

Figure 7-23. New weft is anchored under a minimum of three knot nodes along the same warp.

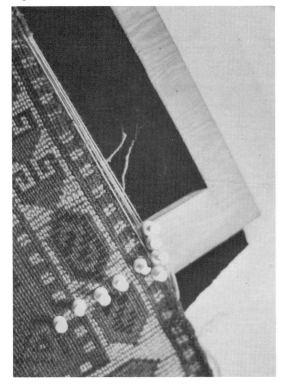

Figure 7-22. Here are new selvage warps attached to pushpins in the frame.

Figure 7-24. New weft is interwoven through a minimum of six sound warps.

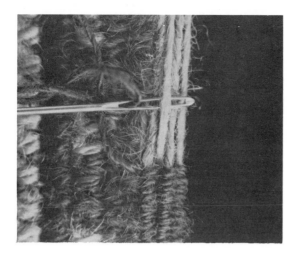

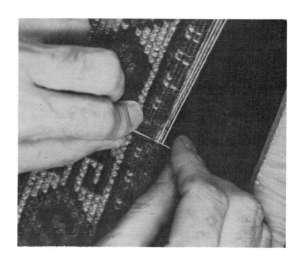

Figure 7-25. The eye of the needle is passed through the open warps.

Figure 7-27. Here the needle is being used to beat down the weft after each pass through the warps. This technique or the use of a comb is essential to weave regular, closely-packed wefts.

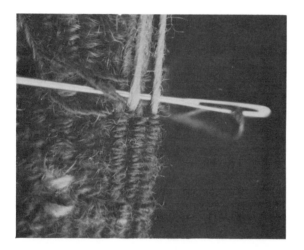

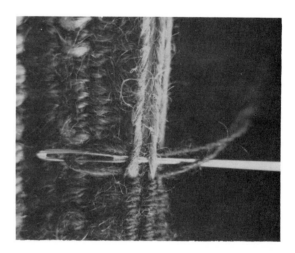

Figure 7-26. Alternate warps are picked up on the needle. The shed will reverse when the needle is moved in the opposite direction. The new weft is woven into the foundation six to nine warps at each point where foundations wefts intersect the selvage warps.

Figure 7-28. The needle direction is reversed. Compare this figure to Figure 7-26.

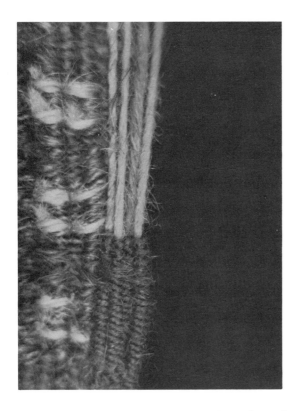

Figure 7-29. Note the regularity and tight packing of the new weft in the selvage.

Figure 7-31. The front of the rug with selvage partially restored.

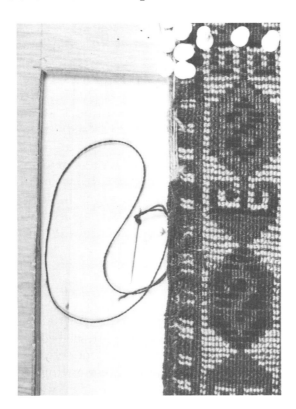

Figure 7-30. The back of the rug with selvage partially restored.

Figure 7-32. The front of the rug with one selvage section completed.

94

## Reconstructing selvage
## next to damaged foundation

The specific repair techniques used to reconstruct foundation, reknot pile and reconstruct selvage are combined where the selvage must be reconstructed and adjacent foundation is damaged. These specific techniques have been described. The necessary steps are performed in this sequence:

1. Mount the rug on a frame large enough to enclose the entire damaged area. The frame should also enclose three inches of sound foundation surrounding the damaged area.

2. Special care is used in mounting the damaged area if there is a deep cut, tear or hole. Warps must line up across the hole and wefts must remain parallel at top and bottom of the hole. Temporary top-to-bottom lacing across the hole may help to stabilize the area during mounting and repair.

3. Rewarp the foundation. Start rewarping next to the sound portion of the foundation and work towards the selvage. Make sure new warp tension is consistent and matches original warp tension.

4. Rewarp the selvage. Leave existing loose selvage warps in place until new selvage warps are anchored.

5. Reweft foundation and selvage. Reknot the pile as rewefting proceeds. Both ground weft and selvage weft are reconstructed at about the same rate.

6. Overcasting is done if appropriate.

## Reconstructing a
## complete selvage

The value of a rug may justify the reconstruction of complete selvages that have been worn away or cut from the rug. Reconstruction of selvage is more difficult and time consuming when ground weft must be restored. If only selvage weft requires restoration, then rebuilding the selvage proceeds much more rapidly. Usually, the total reconstruction of selvage, both selvage weft and ground weft, is practical and worthwhile for smaller rugs only.

Selvage is reconstructed, a section at a time, on a frame about one yard long and one foot wide. The rug is mounted on the frame so there is about six inches between the inside of the frame and the edge to be reselvaged. The rug should be taut (no sagging or wrinkles). The bottom of the rug is at the bottom of the frame. Reselvaging proceeds from the bottom upwards.

A nail is driven into the top and bottom of the frame for each warp in the selvage. These nails may be vertically staggered. Their horizontal spacing determines the width of the selvage. Appropriate selvage width can be found by examining a rug of similar age and origin. Then, space the nails accordingly. The nails at top and bottom must line up so that warps are parallel.

For selvage warps, select a yarn equal to or slightly larger than foundation warps. Each new selvage warp will require a length of yarn at least six inches longer than the overall length of the rug. Tie one end of warp tightly to the bottom nail. The yarn is stretched across the frame, its tension adjusted, and wrapped six times around the opposite nail. Selvage warp tension should equal the tension of warps in the foundation. Note that the extra yarn for each warp is now attached to the nails at the top of the frame. This yarn should be wrapped in hanks or balls to prevent tangling.

Select appropriate yarn for selvage weft and ground weft, if required. Ground weft is anchored in the foundation as described in Chapter 6. The beginning end of selvage weft can be anchored by interweaving it through sound warp. This is the warp shared by both ground weft and selvage weft—the warp that divides the selvage from the foundation.

If both ground weft and selvage weft are used, thread two sharp-pointed needles with the weft. Ground weft and selvage weft are reconstructed across the selvage at the same rate. The needle is moved under alternate warps, reversing direction after passing around the outermost warp. Of course, the shed is reversed as each new weft is woven through the warps. Each new weft is beaten downwards with a segment of a comb.

When the selvage inside the frame is completed, the rug is removed from the frame and remounted so a new portion of the rug edge is set up for reselvaging. The warp nails at the bottom of the frame are removed because the warps are now anchored in the new selvage. However, the new warps must be wrapped around the nails at

the top of the frame after warp tension is adjusted. This process of remounting the rug on the frame is repeated until the selvage is completed.

Selvages are not always straight and parallel. Warp spacing at the bottom end of a rug is maintained by the end beam of the loom. As weaving proceeds away from the beam, warps become more elastic and can be pulled closer together by tight wefts. If the weaver is not careful in adjusting weft tension to keep warps parallel, the top end of the rug will be narrower than the bottom end or the rug will have a "waist", being narrower at the center than at the ends. If there is a waist or curvature in the selvage, this should be reproduced by replacement selvage. Don't attempt to straighten the edge of the rug where there is a basic curve rather than a small local distortion.

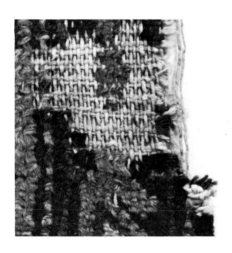

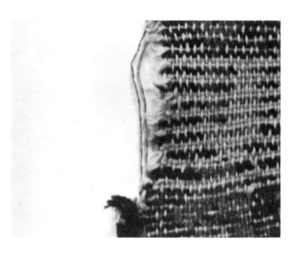

Figure 7-33. Selvage damage to be repaired. The front of the rug. Figures 7-33 through 7-40 show the same rug.
*Provenance:* Hamadan
*Pile:* wool, symmetric knot, 30 knots per sq. in.
*Warp:* cotton, 6-ply, "S" spun overall
*Weft:* cotton, 1 shoot, 6-ply, "S" spun overall

Figure 7-34. The selvage damage from the back of the rug.

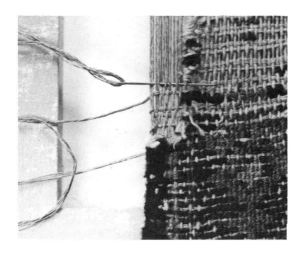

Figure 7-35. Foundation warps are being restored as well as selvage warps. Because the rug is coarsely woven, rewefting can be completed before knots are tied.

Figure 7-37. Foundation repairs, including rewefting, and overcasting are completed and the area is ready for reknotting.

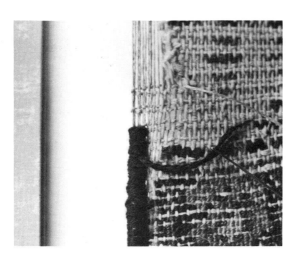

Figure 7-36. Overcasting is done as wefts are completed.

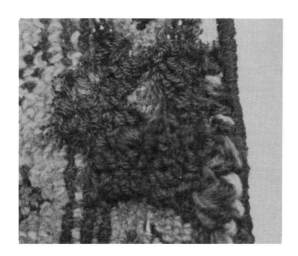

Figure 7-38. New pile knots before trimming.

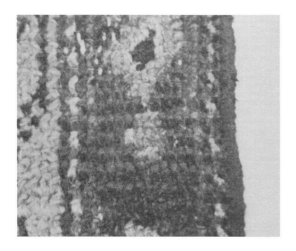

Figure 7-39. The completed repair area from the front of the rug.

Figure 7-41. Foundation repair and selvage reconstruction. Here is the front of a small area under repair. Because the area is small, some rewefting was done before knots were tied. Uncut knot loops are seen on the front of the rug. Note how new ground weft wraps the selvage warps. Additional wrapping is done where rows of knots occur.
*Provenance:* Chinese
*Pile:* wool, asymmetric open to the right, 64 knots per sq. in.
*Warp:* cotton, 9-ply, "S" spun overall
*Weft:* cotton, 2 shoots, 9-ply, "S" spun overall

Figure 7-40. The completed repair area from the back of the rug.

## Adding a false selvage

Whether a false selvage should be used instead of reconstructing selvage depends on the condition of the rug and its value. Most of the selvage of a rug can be lost through wear. In some cases, the original selvage has been cut off. If the considerable time and effort needed for selvage reconstruction is not justified by the post-repair value of such rugs, then a false selvage is the next best alternative. False selvage consists of a center cord that is whip stitched to the rug.

The borders of a rug should be straight and symmetrical. The added selvage is whip stitched to columns of knots at each edge of the rug. Usually, you will need to cut away some edge material so the edge is even and parallel to the column of knots where the whip stitching enters the foundation.

The extent to which edges are cut back is an important decision. You will wish to preserve as much of the rug as possible while selecting a cut-off point that will still provide an aesthetically pleasing border. Usually, there is a guard stripe that will serve satisfactorily as the new border at the edge.

To trim the edge of the rug, work from the back, using an Xacto knife. Be sure that you are cutting *between columns of knots*. Check and recheck as trimming proceeds so that you do not cut wefts between warps held together by pile knots.

At least two columns of knots (four warps) are needed as anchorage for the false selvage. These columns will be concealed by the whip stitching. It's possible to rely on only one column of knots as anchorage for occasional short segments (about six inches) at the edge. The false selvage is built up by stitching extra filler cord in place for these segments.

Yarn selected for whip stitching should match the dominant color of the rug. Yarn for the central cord of the false selvage should be two or three times the size of the foundation warps. Use a sharp pointed needle for whip stitching.

The rug edge is mounted on a frame during whip stitching. But, whip stitching can be done one section at a time. A frame about a yard long can be used and new sections mounted in sequence as work proceeds. Without the frame, the false selvage will be rippled rather than straight.

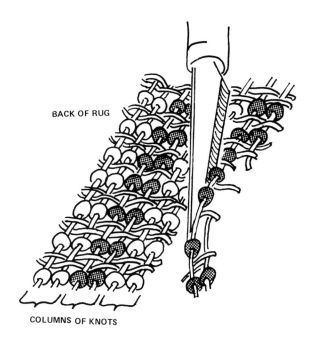

BACK OF RUG

COLUMNS OF KNOTS

Figure 7-42. Trimming a column of knots from the edge of a rug. The cut is made from the back of the rug *between* columns of knots.

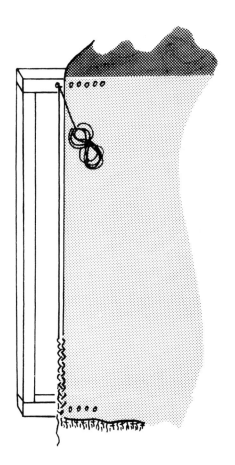

Figure 7-43. A rug mounted on a frame to add a false selvage. Note the extra selvage warp yarn.

After trimming, the starting portion of the rug edge (the bottom of the rug) is mounted on the frame under moderate tension (no sagging or wrinkles) so there is easy access to the edge and both sides. Actual stitching is done from the back of the rug.

A nail is driven into each end of the frame next to the rug edge. The center cord for the false selvage is tied to these nails. The cord is parallel to and immediately next to the rug edge. The tension of the cord matches the tension of the edge warps. Since only a portion of the rug is reselvaged at a time, there will be extra selvage cord (the length of the rug) tied to the upper nail.

Anchor the loose end of the selvage yarn in the same manner as overcasting is anchored. Whip stitch the cord and columns of knots along the edge inside the frame. When the first segment is reselvaged, remove the rug from the frame and remount the rug and center cord for the next segment. The final end of whip stitch yarn is finished in the same manner as overcasting.

## Finishing new selvage or overcasting

Selvage and overcasting receive heavy wear. As a result, fibers or fuzz are usually worn from the exposed yarn in selvages and overcasting. For a new selvage or overcasting to match the rest of the rug in the appearance of age, it may be desirable to remove these fine fibers.

One method is to use hair clippers. Motor driven or manual hair clippers are adjusted to fine cut. These are used to clip the projecting fibers from the selvage or overcasting.

Figure 7-44. This rug was not strictly rectangular so special lacing was needed to mount it on a frame for selvage reconstruction.
*Provenance:* Baluchi
*Pile:* wool, asymmetric open to the left, 72 knots per sq. in.
*Warp:* wool, 2-ply, "S" spun overall
*Weft:* wool, 2 shoots, 2-ply, "S" spun overall

100

# Chapter 8

# Repairing Ends

Structurally, there's no part of a rug that can be more varied than the ends. A whole range of flatweave variations, off loom weaving, and ornamental knotting may be used. Rug ends can be a school of fiber arts. Of necessity, we will describe the repair of only the most common treatments of rug ends.

One treatment of damaged ends is to square off the ends by removing all material above or below a selected foundation weft. This approach has several disadvantages. If the main border is reduced by removing material, then the altered rug will have an unfinished appearance. If only a small area of the end is damaged, it's probably better to invest some effort in reconstruction rather than destroy a substantial portion of the rug for the sake of symmetry.

**Overview of end repair**

Here is an overview of the steps in repairing rug ends:

1. Analyze the end finish.
2. Remove damaged material.
3. Construct a frame.
4. Mount the damaged area on the frame and set up a tension bar.
5. For damage to bottom end, follow this sequence: reconstruct warps, reconstruct bottom end wefts, then reknot and reconstruct foundation wefts.
6. For damage to top end, follow this sequence: reconstruct warps, reknot and reconstruct foundation wefts.
7. Reconstruct special end finishes and stabilize ends.

**Time required for end repairs**

The time required for end repairs is increased by complicated end treatments. A high knot density, producing a high warp count, will increase repair time, as will warp offset. Color changes in the flatweave end will slow repairs. And so will weft locking techniques, fringe knotting and fringe braiding.

As a very approximate guide, assume these repair conditions: a knot density of fifty per square inch, no warp offset, a simple single-color flatweave end, and no weft repair or reknotting in the foundation. Reconstruction of the flatweave end only will require about 15 minutes per warp and about one hour per square inch of flatweave.

**End finish analysis**

End treatments are analyzed so they can be copied in reconstruction. Most end treatments are fairly simple. But, end treatments in village and nomadic rugs may be quite complicated.

All oriental rugs are made with at least several wefts at the ends. These are essential to lock in the top and bottom rows of knots. But beyond these locking wefts, there are many variations in the treatment of ends.

Where a number of wefts (without pile knots) are woven through warps at the end of a rug, a strip of fabric is formed. This strip is referred to as a "webbing", "killim", or "flatweave" end.

We'll describe end treatments in two broad categories. These are end structures made while the rug is still on the loom and end structures made after the rug is removed from the loom. On-loom flatweave ends include:

1. Plain weave
2. Tapestry weaves
   • Slit weave
   • Warp sharing
   • Interlocking wefts
3. Supplementary wefts
   • Supplementary weft float patterning
   • Weft float brocade
4. Weft wrapping
   • Soumak
   • Weft chaining

Off-loom end treatments include:
1. Knotting
2. Braiding
3. Off-loom weaving

Sometimes a number of these end treatments will be combined in a single rug. One way to analyze an end treatment is to unravel a small portion of the damaged material. Trace the paths of selected warps and wefts. With paper and pencil, diagram the structure as you undo it. Then, practice reproducing the structure with spare yarn before you try actual repairs.

*Plain weave.* This is a simple interlacing of one weft per shed through alternate warps. Wefts are continuous from selvage to selvage. The appearance of the fabric is the same from both sides. It is the most common flatweave end for a rug. Wefts may be colored and this produces horizontal stripes in the plain weave.

Figure 8-1. Plain weave. Since neither weft nor warp dominate, this is a balanced plain weave. See Figure 2-38.

*Tapestry weaves.* The following group of flatweaves are tapestry weaves. In general, a tapestry weave is a weft-faced fabric in which wefts are not continuous from selvage to selvage. The weft is reversed in direction a number of times to produce an area of a single color.[1] The wefts in tapestry weaves are structurally essential; the colored wefts used in the design are part of the ground or foundation.

In the *slit weave,* wefts of different colors in the same row reverse direction or turnaround on adjacent warps. If several rows of wefts turnaround on the same warp, then a slit is created in the fabric between warps where the turnarounds occur. This effect is produced where there is a vertical demarcation between areas of different color. If the weft turnarounds are staggered over several adjacent warps, then a diagonal color juncture is created and there is no slit in the fabric.

Figure 8-4. Rewarping of the hole is completed and rewefting has begun.

Figure 8-2. Slit weave. A slit occurs in this type of tapestry weave where wefts reverse direction on adjacent warps. Note the points where wefts reverse direction in the upper portion of the illustration.

Figure 8-5. Here, rewefting is almost completed.

Figure 8-3. This is a damaged slit weave killim. Its structure is similar to that found in the ends of some tribal and nomadic rugs. Weft colors change on adjacent warps. There are slits where there is a change of color with a vertical demarcation.

Figure 8-6. The repaired area is virtually indistinguishable from the surrounding area.

*Warp sharing* occurs when wefts of different colors in the same row reverse direction by looping around the *same* warp. This tapestry weave produces a pinched effect on the turnaround warp. At color junctures, two wefts occupy the same vertical warp space normally filled by only one weft.

Figure 8-7. Warp sharing. In this tapestry weave, wefts of different colors reverse direction on the same warp.

With *interlocking wefts*, differently colored wefts from opposing directions turnaround by looping through each other. There are many variations in this tapestry weave in the manner in which wefts interlock.

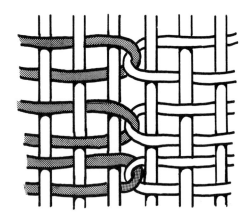

Figure 8-8. Interlocking weft. Wefts of different colors reverse direction by looping through each other.

*Supplementary wefts.*[2] Supplementary wefts are used to create designs or patterns, and are additions to basic weaves. These wefts are not structurally essential to the fabric. Where supplementary wefts are used in rug ends, they are usually added to a plain weave ground. Supplementary wefts are said to "float" where they skip over two or more adjacent warps in a plain weave.

In *supplementary weft float patterning*, supplementary weft floats extend from selvage to selvage. The fabric has a different appearance from each side. One side presents a pattern while the other side reveals the continuation of the supplementary weft yarn between pattern areas or selvages.

*Weft float brocades* are designs created with supplementary wefts that do *not* extend from selvage to selvage. The supplementary wefts weave back and forth in a limited area or are cut. Here, too, the pattern side of the fabric has a different appearance than the back. There are many variations in the use of supplementary wefts. Repairs require a careful anaysis to reproduce the existing structure.

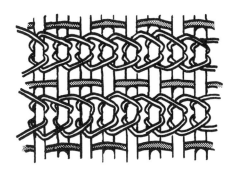

*Weft wrapping.* In weft wrapping, the weft regularly loops around warps. There are many weft wrapping structures. Two of the most common in oriental rugs are soumak and weft chaining. Technically, pile knotting is weft wrapping with a discontinuous supplementary weft. But here, we are dealing with weft wrapping with a continuous weft.

*Soumak* is weft wrapping with a supplementary weft. Soumak is similar to tapestry weaves in that the colored weft does not extend from selvage to selvage but is used to create colored areas. Unlike tapestry weaves, the colored weft is supplementary rather than a ground weft. A crochet hook, tapestry needle or small shuttle can be used to weave soumak wefts through and around the warps.

Basically, soumak is weft looping through warps with unequal numbers of warps gathered in a forward loop and a backward loop. The weft moves across the warps in the direction of the loops gathering the larger number of warps. For example, the weft loops once around each warp: two warps forward and one warp back. Note the angle of the soumak loop from the top of the flatweave. By reversing the direction of soumak looping with the next weft, a characteristic herringbone effect is created.

Figure 8-9. Soumak. Ground wefts are dark. Supplementary wefts are light. Here, the soumak weft loops backwards around a single warp and forwards around two warps. Other combinations of loop are used such as two warps backwards and four warps forward.

To outline areas, soumak wefts can run vertically or diagonally. Where soumak wefts are vertical, they loop around ground wefts. Where they are diagonal, they loop around the intersections of ground wefts and warps.

Figure 8-10. The black areas in this Caucasian soumak are badly etched. Note the boteh.
*Provenance:* Caucasian soumak
*Warp:* wool, 3-ply, "Z" spun overall
*Weft:* wool, single, "Z" spun

Figure 8-11. Damaged weft has been removed from the boteh.

Figure 8-13. The black boteh is completely restored.

Figure 8-12. The boteh is partly restored using the soumak technique.

*Weft chaining* is a form of weft wrapping basically similar to crochet work, where one loop is pulled through another. Weft chaining is rarely used as an all-over flatweave, but it is used to lock the last weft of a plain weave end in place. Accordingly, weft chaining is described as a method of stabilizing flatwoven ends in the last part of this chapter.

If warp ends are left untreated, they tend to fray and usage unravels the last wefts in the flatweave end of the rug. To prevent this unraveling, there is a variety of ways of finishing warps after the rug is taken from the loom. These structures include knotting, braiding and offloom weaving.

*Knotting.* Two or more warps can be knotted together and forced against the last weft as the knot is tightened. A single overhand knot is adequate. Often, pairs of warps are knotted together, four warps making up the knot.

When more than two warps are tied for the knot, and usually more than two warps are knotted, the farthest warp tied in the knot should crossover the farthest warp tied in the next knot as shown. Otherwise, the tension of the knots will tend to spread the warps between knots. Knotted meshwork is created with rows of staggered knots.

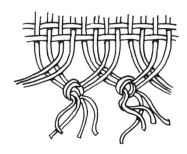

Figure 8-14. Knotted fringe. Note how pairs of warps overlap to prevent warp spreading between warp knots.

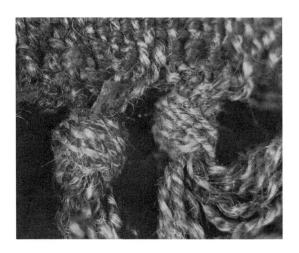

Figure 8-15. A plain weave end that has been knotted.

*Braiding.* Warps can be braided to finish the end. When this is done, some type of knot is tied at the end of the braid to prevent it from unraveling. The common braid can be made with three warps or three groups of warps, as shown.

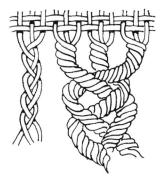

Figure 8-16. Braided warps. Single warps can be braided or groups of warps can be braided.

*Off-loom weaving.* Off-loom weaving is closely related to braiding. Only warps are used to create a type of flatweave.

One method of weaving starts with a warp at one edge which is interlaced with the remaining warps up against the last weft. The next warp is similarly interlaced and so on as shown. This woven end has several distinctive features. Warp ends return towards the rug on the underside of the resulting flatweave. Also, left and right edges of the flatweave will have a different character. One edge has a finished appearance while the other edge has projecting warps that must be knotted.

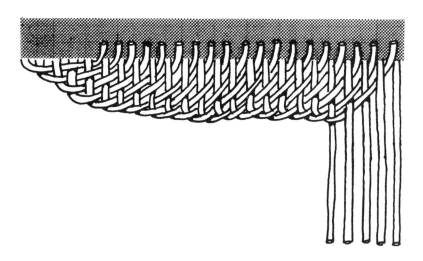

Figure 8-17. Off-loom weaving. Here, warps are interwoven. An example of this end treatment is shown in Figure 2-42.

Figure 8-18. Off-loom weaving end treatment.
*Provenance:* Hamadan
*Pile:* wool, symmetric knot, 48 knots per sq. in.
*Warp:* cotton, 3-ply, "S" spun overall
*West:* cotton, 1 shoot, single "S" spun

## Preparing the damaged area for repair

Damaged end material is unreliable anchorage for new warps and wefts and should be cut away. It's also best to simplify, and thus shorten, the outline of the reconstructed area. This minimizes the signs of reconstruction and can save a little time in repair work. Of course, the advantages of removing irregular areas of sound material must be weighed against the goal of preserving original rug material.

In removing or cutting back broken or stretched wefts, leave a half-inch stub projecting from under the crossing warp. This stub will be pulled taut when the weft is rewoven. Damaged or distorted warps are left in place until they are about to be replaced with new warp.

After damaged material is removed, there should be at least one sound weft bordering the cleared area. Stubs of old warp will project over or under this weft.

## Constructing a frame with tension bar

A frame is constructed large enough to enclose the damaged area and about three inches of sound material at the top and sides of the damaged area. The enclosed area must allow space for the warp fringe with an additional inch clearance. Assume the damaged foundation is two inches deep and three inches wide and the flatweave and warp fringe are two inches wide. Then the frame must enclose an area of about nine by eight inches.

Since new warps must be kept under tension as reknotting and rewefting proceed, they are tied to or pass around a tension bar. The tension bar is a piece of metal bar stock or rod approximately one-eighth to one-quarter inch in diameter. The bar is tied to nails driven into the top or bottom edge of the frame. It spans the width of the frame. Strong cord or twine is used to tie the bar to the nails. The nails are spaced about three inches apart. When the rug is mounted on the frame, the ties can be adjusted so the bar is parallel to the wefts in the rug.

One end of the twine is tied to the old fringe warp and the other end of the twine is tied to the tension bar. Adjust these ties so tension is even across all of the old warps tied to the tension bar.

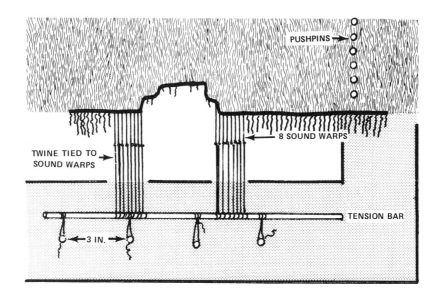

Figure 8-19. Diagram of rug end mounted using a tension bar.

## Mounting the rug on the frame

The end of the rug to be repaired is mounted next to the tension bar on the frame. About one-half to one inch of space is left between the end of the warp fringe and the tension bar. The rug is mounted with wefts parallel to the tension bar, using pushpins or carpet tacks spaced about one inch apart. There should be no sagging or tension wrinkles.

The rug is held taut along the warps during repair. To do this, eight old fringe warps on either side of the repair area are tied to the tension bar. The fringe warps selected should be whole and sound. This creates a band of warp-wise tension on either side of the repair area. These old warps will also provide anchorage for new wefts. Pieces of twine are used to extend these old warps.

If there is no old warp fringe remaining, then the rug end can be temporarily laced to the tension bar on either side of a selected repair area. The warp-wise span of the lacing must be somewhat longer than the depth of foundation reconstruction plus fringe length.

## Rewarping ends

The knot density of the rug determines the rewarping procedure to be used. If knot density is greater than about one hundred knots per square inch, rewarping is done only from the field towards the end. Each new warp is separately anchored in the foundation and tied to the tension bar.

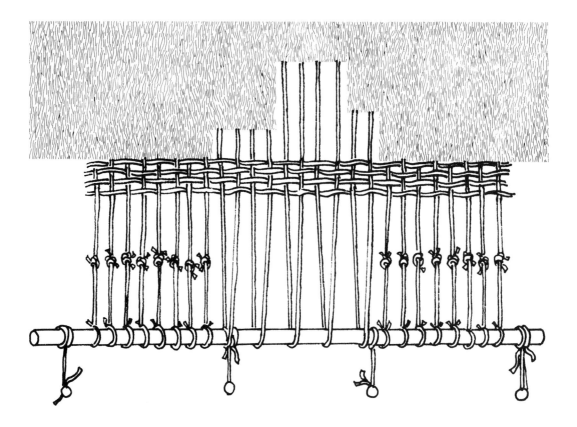

Figure 8-20. Here, a rug end is mounted, rewarped and a plain weave end woven before reknotting. The new warps re-enter the rug after passing around the tension bar. If warp spacing were very fine, each new warp would be tied to the tension bar.

However, if knot density is lower than about one hundred knots per square inch, then the new warp can loop around the tension bar, re-enter the foundation, turn around on the adjacent old warp, return to loop around the tension bar, and so on.

In rewarping ends, most of the rewarping guidelines with which you are familiar are followed.

- Select yarn of a type and color to match old yarn. New warp yarn may be slightly smaller than old warp yarn.
- Wax the new warp yarn.
- Use a sharp pointed needle with the smallest eye that will accept the yarn.
- By guiding the needle, make sure new warps lie directly on top (from the back of the rug) of old warps and not to either side.

- Carefully match new warp tension with old warp tension.
- Stagger new warp anchoring knots or turnarounds in the foundation.

We'll assume that the end to be restored is the bottom of the rug. This is the procedure for anchoring the first new warp. Identify a damaged warp adjacent to a sound old warp. Count seven knot nodes above the border weft on this old warp. This is the entry point for the needle. Pass the needle under three knot nodes on the old warp. Pull the new warp yarn to the surface after it passes under three knot nodes, leaving a one-inch tail or stub above the seventh knot node.

Tie a knot in the new warp yarn close to the surface of the rug. Reinsert the needle where it emerged and pass the needle under the four remaining knot nodes. Pull the yarn tight so the anchoring knot above the

110

fourth knot node is snug against the surface. Pull on the tail of the new warp yarn above the seventh knot node and clip it flush with the back of the rug. The end of the first new warp is now anchored in the foundation.

If the rug is tightly woven, above one hundred knots per square inch, then the remaining end of the new warp is tied to the tension bar after adjusting new warp tension to match old warp tension. Each new warp is anchored in this same manner, only the location of the anchoring knot in the new warp is staggered between the third and sixth knot node. This avoids the formation of a ridge of knots along the same weft.

If the rug has a knot density of less than about one hundred knots per square inch, then the new warp yarn is looped around the tension bar. The needle is inserted under the knot node at the edge of the repair area on the adjacent old warp. The old warp stub is pulled taut while the needle is worked under three to six knot nodes. Tension is then adjusted for the first two new warps before the needle is returned again on an adjacent old warp. The turnarounds in the foundation are staggered to prevent a ridge from forming.

Use an anchoring knot in the new warp yarn to anchor it in the foundation if the last new warp returns into the foundation. If the last new warp comes *from* the foundation, then it must be tied to the tension bar.

### Rewefting ends

After rewarping, the initial steps in rewefting depend on whether the bottom end or top end of the rug is being repaired. For repairs at the top end, reknotting and rewefting is completed before a flatweave end or locking wefts are woven. But, for repairs at the bottom end, locking wefts or a flatweave end must be woven before pile knots can be tied on foundation warps.

These are the guidelines to be followed in rewefting:

- Match new weft yarn with existing weft in type, size and color.
- Use a sharp pointed needle with the smallest eye that will accept the new weft yarn.
- Anchor new wefts on warps as described in Chapter 6.
- Push old weft ends in the flatweave to the back of the rug.
- Push old weft ends in the foundation to the front of the rug.
- Copy the path of old wefts through warp sheds.
- Reproduce existing weft tension with new wefts. Duplicate cable and sinuous wefts.
- Use a comb segment to beat wefts down.

In the following discussion, we'll assume repairs must be made to the bottom of a rug with a narrow flatweave end.

Working from the back of the rug, the first (and bottom) new weft is anchored on an old warp on either side of the damaged area. If possible, this old warp is the third or fourth sound warp from the damaged area. The needle points to the bottom of the rug in anchoring the new weft under about eight old wefts that cross the old warp. Do not use an anchoring knot in the new weft as you would use in anchoring a warp.

After anchoring the first weft, rewefting of the flatweave is done from the front of the rug. The new weft is woven across the damaged area through the old warps, then new warps, then three or four old warps on the other side of the damaged area. The new weft passes through the same shed as the old weft it is replacing. After tension is adjusted, the new weft reverses direction by looping around the fourth or fifth old warp. These turnarounds are staggered.

Use the point of the needle to anchor new weft in the sound portion of the flatweave. Use the eye-end of the needle to carry new weft through warps only.

About three new wefts are woven before wefts can be beaten down. Thereafter, each new weft is beaten down. As new wefts are woven, adjust the tension and vertical weft density so the texture of the new flatweave matches that of the old flatweave. The weaving should be neat and regular. Pull old weft stubs to the back of the flatweave as weaving proceeds. When the flatweave end is finished, these are clipped flush with the surface. When the uppermost weft of the flatweave end is completed, pile knots are tied and rewefting and reknotting proceed as described in Chapter 6.

Rugs that will not be subjected to heavy usage require no further end treatment, assuming that a flatweave end only is an appropriate and tasteful finish. If the rug will receive heavy usage, then either weft chaining or knotted fringes are needed. The rug is left on the frame for weft chaining.

## Appearance of reconstructed flatweave ends

By close examination, one can see signs of restoration on the front of a flatweave even though it has been carefully rewoven. There is some irregularity evident at the edges of the restored area. These signs of reconstruction are minimized by:

- Eliminating irregularities in the outline or border of the repair area by removing some sound material where necessary.
- Using weft yarn of matching size, type and color.
- Consistently selecting the appropriate shed for each new weft.
- Staggering new weft turnarounds.
- Reproducing the vertical weft packing or looseness of the original weave.
- Pulling all weft stubs in the flatweave to the back of the rug as work proceeds.

## End stitching or stabilizing

Only a few wefts may remain at the end of a rug to lock the first row of pile knots in place. This occurs when damaged material is removed to square off the ends of a rug on a selected weft or when reconstruction of a flatweave end is not worthwhile.

If fringe warps are long enough they can be knotted to hold the wefts in place. However, a long fringe is not likely, so end stitching is often used to lock the wefts and stabilize the end. On the front of the rug, the stitching is concealed by pile. This concealment is slightly more successful at the bottom end than at the top end.

For stitching, use a heavy duty linen or cotton thread. Do not use nylon thread since this has a tendency to cut through other fibers. The thread should have the same hue as end knots or wefts. An exact color match is not critical as it is for pile yarn. Work from the back of the rug. Use a sharp pointed needle and knot the thread at the loose end. Each stitch binds the end wefts and a minimum of two rows of knots.

The two most common stitches are the simple whip stitch and the buttonhole stitch. Here are the steps in using the *whip stitch.*

Insert the needle between two warps and above the weft above the second row of knots. Draw the thread through so the knot is seated against the back of the rug. Loop around the end of the rug so the loop of thread lies between the same warps where the knot is seated. On the front of the rug, the thread should lie in the cleft between columns of knots without trapping any pile or fringe warps.

Reinsert the needle from the back of the rug, two to eight warps to the right above the same weft where the knot is seated. Stitch spacing depends on pile knot density. At higher knot densities, more warps can be skipped. When the stitch is drawn tight, check the front of the rug to be sure pile is

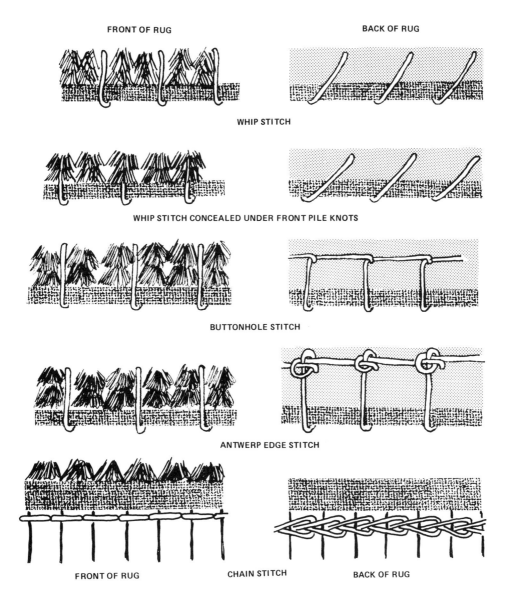

FRONT OF RUG                    BACK OF RUG

WHIP STITCH

WHIP STITCH CONCEALED UNDER FRONT PILE KNOTS

BUTTONHOLE STITCH

ANTWERP EDGE STITCH

FRONT OF RUG          CHAIN STITCH          BACK OF RUG

Figure 8-21. End stitches. Here are a variety of
stitches used to stabilize rug ends by keeping end
wefts from unraveling.

not trapped under the stitch. Diagonal stitches are visible from the back of the rug. Stitches on the front of the rug lie between warps and are hidden by pile.

A variation of the whip stitch does a better job of concealing the stitch from the front of the rug. Thread is inserted under the knot loops and above a warp from the *front* of the rug, instead of allowing the stitch to lie between columns of knots. This variation also does a better job of locking the stitches in place if the thread should part when the rug is in use. Stitch spacing is one-quarter to one-half inch.

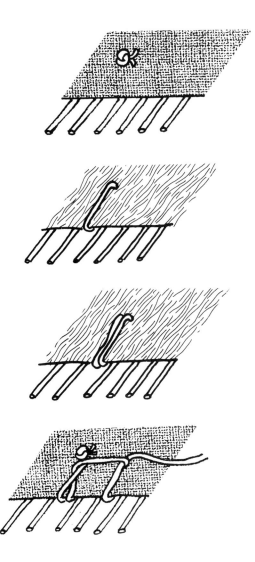

Figure 8-22. Steps in beginning the buttonhole stitch. First, the back of the rug is shown with the knot seated against it. Then, there are two views of the front of the rug showing the initial loops around the rug end. Finally, the back of the rug is shown with two complete stitches.

Here are the steps in using the *button-hole stitch.*

Insert the needle from the back of the rug between two warps and above the weft above the second row of pile knots. Draw the thread through so the knot is seated against the back of the rug. Bring the thread around the end so it lies between the two warps where the knot is seated. Reinsert the needle at the same point and bring it around the end again in the same way.

Slip the needle under the stitch on the back of the rug from right to left. Insert the needle two to eight warps to the right above the same weft where the knot is seated. The needle is inserted between two warps. Draw the thread through and a diagonal stitch is formed. Bring the thread around the end of the rug between the same two warps where the needle was just inserted. Pass the needle under the diagonal stitch from right to left and draw the thread tight. The loops of thread should now lie neatly between two warps. The stitch is continued in this manner until the end weft is locked in place.

The buttonhole stitch can be modified by tying a knot at the point where the second stitch passes under the prior stitch. This form is known as the Antwerp edge. Because of the knots, this stitching will not unravel if it is broken at some point.

A *crochet stitch or weft chaining* is also used to finish rug ends. Basically, it amounts to pulling one loop through another with a crochet hook after one end of the yarn is tied to an edge warp. Two or more fringe warps are enclosed by each stitch. From the back of the rug, the interlocking loops are evident. From the front of the rug, only a single line of stitches can be seen. This chain stitch binds the warps tightly. However, it can unravel quickly if it is broken or an end is free.

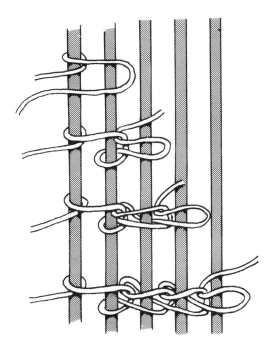

Figure 8-23. Steps in starting the chain stitch.

Figure 8-25. The back of the same rug showing the damaged area.

Figure 8-24. The damaged portion of the top end of a rug to be repaired. The repair is shown in Figures 8-24 through 8-40.
*Provenance:* Hamadan
*Pile:* wool, symmetric knot, 30 knots per sq. in.
*Warp:* cotton, 6-ply, "S" spun overall
*Weft:* cotton, 1 shoot, 6-ply, "S" spun overall

Figure 8-26. Here is the rug mounted on the frame and partially rewarped. A knitting needle, braced by nails, serves as a tension bar.

Figure 8-27. The rewarped damaged area from the front of the rug.

Figure 8-29. Because this is a coarsely woven rug, it is possible to reweft without tying the pile knots as rewefting proceeds. Here, rewefting is partially completed.

Figure 8-28. The rewarped damaged area from the back of the rug.

Figure 8-30. This is the front of the rug with rewefting completed.

Figure 8-31. A single row of soumak stitches has been woven along the outer edge of the damaged area to stabilize the end and make it compatible with the rug end on either side.

Figure 8-33. Here is the partially reknotted area from the back of the rug.

Figure 8-32. Reknotting has begun in the rewefted area closest to the body of the rug. Since this is the top end. knots and weft will be beaten down towards the sound area.

Figure 8-34. Reknotting is almost completed.

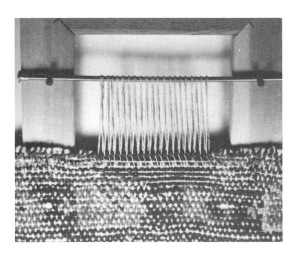

Figure 8-35. Reknotting is complete, but the last rows of knots are untrimmed.

Figure 8-37. Here is the back of the rug with whip stitching in place.

Figure 8-36. The back of the rug with reknotting completed.

Figure 8-38. The front of the rug before trimming the new warp ends.

Figure 8-39. The finished repair from the front.

Figure 8-41. A corner repair on a Caucasian rug.

Figure 8-40. The back of the rug after repair.

Figure 8-42. Note how twine has been used to place old and new warps under tension. Reknotting has started.

Figure 8-43. The completed repair from the front.

## False fringes

False fringes can be purchased and sewn to the ends of rugs. The problem with this practice is that false fringes appear false. The alternatives of reconstruction or squaring-off the ends are both preferable to the artificial appearance of a false fringe. When an inexpensive rug is to be returned to use, damaged ends can be squared-off and overcast in the same manner as the selvedge.

## Solving repair problems

Every possible rug defect cannot be covered in a single text on repairs. Special reconstruction problems are bound to occur. These problems are usually solvable by adapting the techniques we have described to the particular circumstances.

Your ingenuity can be challenged by such problems. Take your time in settling on a solution. Often, the first solution that occurs to you will not be the best one. Think all of the repair steps through to the conclusion before you take any action.

One type of repair problem arises from the need to keep a damaged foundation area under even tension during structural repairs. The shapes, sizes and locations of damage are variable. Yet, in all cases, even tension must be provided. In resolving this problem, remember that a damaged area can be stabilized by temporary stitching and lacing and that lacing can be used to attach the rug to a frame. Virtually all tensioning problems can be solved by some type of adjustable lacing system.

1. P. Collingwood, *The Techniques of Rug Weaving*, Watson-Guptill, 1978, p.141
2. J.T. Wertime, *Flat-Woven Structures Found in Nomadic and Village Weavings from the Near East and Central Asia*, Textile Museum Journal, 1979, p.39

# Chapter 9

# Washing Rugs and Stain Removal

Why wash a rug? A clean rug has brighter, clearer colors and the wool is glossier. If this isn't reason enough, washing a rug protects it. When a soiled rug is used, soil particles cut the fibers and accelerate wear. If a rug is to be stored, then washing a rug helps protect it from carpet beetles, moths and mildew. Another motive is to discover the rug's true condition. The first washing of a newly acquired rug may disclose virtues and faults. One may discover brilliant colors and attractive design details or painted areas and permanent stains. Ultimately, the truth is best.

When a rug is washed, what is it that's washed from the rug? According to a research survey of American households,[1] soil on surfaces in the home consists of:

45% sand and clays
12% animal protein fibers
12% cellulose fibers
10% alcohol-soluble particles (resins, gums, fatty acids)
 6% ether-soluble particles (fats, oils, rubber, asphalt)
 5% gypsum
 5% limestone
 3% moisture
 2% miscellaneous

Usually, the combination of the solvent action of the detergent and the mechanical action of the washing process are sufficient to remove this collection of substances.

Conservators regard washing a fabric as an irreversible process. A rug can be permanently affected—adversely affected by washing. Generally, the risk is worthwhile. But it's best to understand and evaluate the risk before the rug goes into the bath.

**The risks in washing**

One risk is running or bleeding colors. This risk is greatest where there are large areas of white or light-colored pile or white areas next to red or orange colored pile. Are there presently signs of running or bleeding in light-colored areas? If so, it could happen again. Before washing, test for color fastness. Use a clean, white fabric moistened with a solution of detergent and water. Rub *each color* vigorously to see if any color transfers to the test cloth. This test is important. A rug can be ruined if light-colored areas are stained with other colors.

If the test cloth picks up a lot of color, do not wash the rug. Do not attempt to wash all-silk rugs. Colors are very likely to run or wash out and the silk will lose glossiness. Send the rug to a specialist in stain removal if it is silk or tests indicate colors may run.

If there is only a very light transfer of color to the test cloth, then there is still some risk in washing the rug. The following table will help you evaluate that risk. *CAUTION:* This table should be used only if there is a light transfer of color to the test cloth.

Shrinking is an unlikely possibility. Rugs are washed and rinsed in water at room temperature so shrinking should not be a problem. Even if it does occur, the shrinkage will only be slight (and the result will be a higher knot density). However, rugs can change shape after washing. They may be slightly narrower at the top end. A rug could be in this trapezoidal shape when it was taken from the loom. After initial washing, it may have been stretched into a rectangular shape as it dried. The subsequent washing permits the rug to return to its original shape.

Washing can fix or set certain stains. This is prevented by spot stain removal before washing. Washing removes any sizing in new rugs. When sizing or starch has been added to a rug to increase its bulk and stiffness, the rug will be comparatively soft and limp after washing.

| Color of Rug | Only light colors tranfer in test | Dark colors transfer in test |
|---|---|---|
| Rug has light colors only | Running possible, but serious damage unlikely | Not applicable |
| Rug has dark colors only | Not applicable | Running possible |
| Predominantly light colors with a few dark areas | Running possible, but serious damage unlikely | Running possible |
| Predominantly dark colors with a few light areas | Running possible, but serious damage unlikely | Running probable |

If the rug has suffered dry rot or is brittle with age, washing will tend to disintegrate the damaged area. The condition should be carefully assessed before washing a rug that may have a fragile foundation. See Chapter 3, "Mildew and rot." If brittle or rotted areas are small and reconstruction is intended, then washing may be desirable. When there will be no reconstruction and the foundation is brittle, then the rug should not be washed, only surface cleaned.

After washing, white knots where warps have been tied together may be noticeable from the front of the rug. Some dealers use felt tip pens to paint warp knots so they are less apparent. When the ink washes out, the knots can be seen. Sometimes the white cotton warp fringe will turn light brown as the rug dries after washing. Usually, this problem is cleared up by an additional thorough washing of the fringe. Minimize wetting adjacent pile so there is no "wick" effect in the fringe washing.

## Preparing the rug for washing

Before washing, inspect the rug carefully. Look for caked soil, paint, stains, dry rot and damaged areas. Caked soil should be broken up and removed with a dull table knife. Paint and stains should be removed as described later in this chapter. Damaged areas that might tear or unravel during washing are stopped off. That is, damaged ends or sides are temporarily stitched up. Holes and other damaged areas can be strengthened for washing by rough stitching white fabric patches to them.

The rug is vacuum cleaned. Use a small vacuum nozzle without brush so there is maximum suction. First, vacuum the back of the rug. After vacuuming the back, you'll probably find sand and dirt on the floor that was loosened from the pile. If there's a lot of this material, it's a good idea to vacuum the back again. Then, carefully vacuum the front of the rug.

## Washing, rinsing and drying

Household detergents are unsatisfactory for washing rugs. It's too difficult to rinse out the suds and detergent. Use a mild industrial detergent with a pH of less than 7.5. A good detergent is "Orvus W A Paste." This is sodium lauryl sulphate. The product is biodegradable and manufactured by Proctor and Gamble. It is sold by commercial laundry and cleaning supply companies. Orvus is used by veterinarians to wash pets. If it's gentle enough for old Shep, it's gentle enough for your rug.

Mix about one cup of Orvus with about 15 to 20 gallons of water for the washing solution. If there's a high mineral content in your water supply, a water softener helps the cleaning action. Only cold or room-temperature water should be used for washing and rinsing.

The rug is completely immersed and soaked in the washing solution for about one hour. Agitating the rug every fifteen minutes is helpful. By the time the rug has soaked one-half hour, one can see a considerable amount of soil released into the wash water.

A large rug can be accordion folded into the washing solution. For a larger rug, so folded, washing time should be increased to two hours with a rinse and new washing solution after one hour. In agitating a folded rug, lift up the folds one at a time on either side so wash water circulates between the folds.

After soaking, the rug is scrubbed vigorously on both sides with a stiff fiber brush, the type available in hardware stores for hand-scrubbing floors. The rug is then rinsed until rinse water runs clear. A large rug should be spread out, back up, and rinsed by hosing it down. Then, it is reversed and the front of the rug hosed down. Rinsing must be very thorough.

A wet rug is very heavy. Two strong people will be needed to handle a wet nine-by-twelve rug. Wet rugs must be supported carefully in handling. The weight of the water-logged rug can cause the rug to tear if it is supported only by one edge. Do not stress damaged areas in handling the rug when it is wet.

When rinsing is complete, the rug is spread out, pile upwards, and water is forced from the rug with a squeegee. This is the same type of squeegee used to wash windows—a thick rubber strip fixed in a bracket with a handle. The squeegee is moved in the direction of the pile; starting at the top of the rug and working towards the bottom. This should be done three times. The more water forced from the rug, the sooner the rug will dry. If possible, the rug is allowed to dry while it lies flat. Drying time depends on the rug condition, size and ambient temperature and humidity. Typically, a nine-by-twelve rug in full pile will require between two and three days to dry completely.

## Washing small fragile rugs

Rugs that are brittle, crumbling or powdering should not be washed. However small rugs that are fragile can be washed using special equipment.

Frames are built and covered with plastic window screening. The rug is placed on one screen and the two screens are laced together, sandwiching the rug between them. The screens and rug are emersed in the wash solution and very gently agitated. After soaking, the rug is rinsed in several baths and allowed to dry while remaining on one of the screens.

Whether to wash a rug is always a matter of judgment. This judgment is especially important if the rug is both fragile and very valuable. In such cases, it's best to have the rug washed by a professional textile conservator.

## Restoring lanolin or wool fat to rugs

As rugs age and are washed again and again, the natural lanolin in the wool fibers is lost. Since lanolin helps make wool glossy, its loss may leave the wool dull and lusterless. This lanolin can be restored. However, the treatment should be considered only for rugs that have been thoroughly washed and that still have a dull and lifeless appearance after drying. The addition of lanolin should not be done automatically.

Obtain pure hydrous lanolin. This is available at drug stores. Make sure the lanolin is *hydrous,* otherwise it cannot be dispersed in solution. A solution of dispersed lanolin is prepared. This is done by adding one heaping tablespoon of hydrous lanolin to two cups of boiling water. In another container, thoroughly mix one tablespoon of Orvus or other mild liquid detergent and two cups of water. Now, mix the two solutions together. A milky solution will result. There is some tendency for the lanolin to separate, but agitating the mixture re-disperses the lanolin.

This solution is applied to a clean rug after it is rinsed and squeegeed, but before it has dried. Thoroughly moisten a sponge with the solution, rubbing it into the pile, a square foot at a time. First, work the sponge against the pile direction, and then with the pile direction. Finishing strokes are in the direction of the pile. The objective is a thin, even coating of all the fibers in the pile. The solution is also applied to the back of the rug.

## Surface cleaning rugs

Surface cleaning is much less satisfactory than immersion washing. But, in some situations, it may not be possible to wash the rug by immersion or the rug may be too fragile for immersion washing.

After testing for color fastness, mix a strong solution of Orvus and water and agitate the solution so suds are formed. With a sponge, rub the suds only into the pile, a square foot at a time. Rinse the sponge frequently so that soil picked up by the sponge is released in another container of water. As each area is finished, moisten the sponge with clean water and wipe the pile downwards towards the bottom of the rug. No free water should be released into the pile or foundation during surface cleaning. Let the rug dry flat.

## Stain removal

There's a very large range of dyes used in rugs. This range includes vegetable dyes, analine dyes, azo dyes and chrome dyes. Usually, the specific rug dye is not identified in stain removal. As a result, the effect of the stain removal process on the dyes in the rug is not entirely predictable. There's a definite risk of damaging the rug through stain removal techniques. The techniques can cause colors to fade or bleed, or dull glossy fibers or even weaken fibers in the rug.

The risk of damage is minimized by testing. Always test the stain removal procedure on a small area on the back of the rug. Only by testing can you be sure you are not making a bad condition worse.

An excellent reference for stain removal is *Removing Stains from Fabrics*, Home and Garden Bulletin, No. 62, United States Department of Agriculture. Most of the following stain removal procedures are from this source. First, stain removal supplies are described, then the basic manual techniques for removing stains, then the specific procedures for removing eight groups of staining substances.

## Stain removal supplies

Most of these items are ordinary household supplies. Substitutes are suggested for a few materials that may be difficult to obtain. Follow carefully all precautions for the storage and use of hazardous chemicals.

*Absorbent materials:* You will need an ample supply of clean absorbent materials, such as absorbent cotton, white paper towels, white facial tissues and soft white cotton cloths. Sponges are also useful, but test them with stain removers to be sure they can withstand the chemicals.

*Alcohol:* Use rubbing alcohol or denatured alcohol (70 or 90 percent concentration). Do not use alcohol with added color or fragrances. Alcohol fades some dyes, so test the rug for color fastness before using alcohol on a stain. Caution: alcohol is poisonous and flammable. Observe all precautions on the label.

*Ammonia:* Use household ammonia diluted with an equal amount of water. Do not use ammonia with added color or fragrances. Ammonia changes the color of some dyes. To restore the color, rinse the color-changed area thoroughly with water and apply a few drops of white vinegar. Rinse well with water again.

Caution: Poisonous. Avoid inhaling ammonia fumes. Ammonia will cause burns or irritation if it comes in contact with the skin or eyes. Observe all precautions on the label.

*Amyl acetate:* Amyl acetate (banana oil) is sold in drug stores. Ask for "chemically pure amyl acetate." If you cannot obtain amyl acetate, you may substitute fingernail polish remover. Do not use oily-type polish remover.

Caution: Amyl acetate is poisonous and flammable. Do not breathe the vapors. Amyl acetate is a strong solvent for plastics. Do not allow it to come in contact with plastics or furniture finishes.

*Coconut oil:* Coconut oil is sold in drug stores and health food stores. It is used in combination with a solvent. If you cannot obtain coconut oil, you may substitute mineral oil, which is almost as effective.

*Drycleaning solvent:* Drycleaning solvent is sold in variety stores, hardware stores and grocery stores. It may contain any or all of these ingredients: petroleum solvent; petroleum hydrocarbon; petroleum distillate; 1, 1, 1, trichloroethane; perchloroethylene; or Varsol.

Caution: Do not use drycleaning solvent around flame or where sparking may occur. Use where there is ample fresh air circulating. Do not inhale fumes and avoid contact with skin. Observe precautions on the label.

*Dry spotter:* To prepare dry spotter, mix one part coconut oil and eight parts drycleaning solvent. This solution is used to remove many kinds of stains. Dry spotter keeps well if the container is tightly capped to prevent evaporation of the drycleaning solvent. If you cannot obtain coconut oil, use mineral oil in the same amount as coconut oil.

Caution: Dry spotter is poisonous and may be flammable. Follow all precautions given for drycleaning solvent.

*Enzyme product:* Use an enzyme presoak. This product may be stored as purchased, but becomes inactive if stored after it is made into a solution.

*Glycerine:* Glycerine is sold in drug stores. It is used to prepare "wet spotter" which is used to remove many kinds of stains. It is used to remove ballpoint ink stains.

*Sodium thiosulfate:* Use pure sodium thiosulfate or "fixer" sold in drug stores and photo supply stores. Do not use photo fixer solution that contains other chemicals in addition to sodium thiosulfate. Sodium thiosulfate is used to remove iodine stains.

*Hydrogen peroxide:* Use a 3-percent solution sold as a mild antiseptic. Don't use the stronger solution sold in cosmetic departments for bleaching hair. Hydrogen peroxide should be stored in a cool dark place. It loses strength when stored for extended periods of time.

Bleach that contains sodium perborate or "oxygen-type" bleach may be substituted for hydrogen peroxide, although it is slower acting. Very thorough rinsing is needed to remove this type of bleach.

Do not use or store hydrogen peroxide or oxygen-type bleach in metal containers or use it with metal objects. Metal may speed up action of the bleach enough to cause fiber damage. Also, metal in contact with hydrogen peroxide or bleach may tarnish and cause additional stains on fabrics.

*Vinegar:* Use white vinegar; colored vinegar can leave a stain. If a dye changes color after vinegar has been used, rinse the color-changed area thoroughly with water and add a few drops of ammonia. Then rinse well with water again.

*Wet spotter:* Prepare wet spotter by mixing one part glycerine, one part Orvus or mild liquid detergent and eight parts water. Shake well before each use. This mixture is used to remove many kinds of stains.

## Stain removal techniques

The working surface for stain removal should be a hard surface of a material that will not be affected by any of the chemicals used. A heavy glass pie pan turned upside down makes a good working surface. A table or countertop should be protected from spilled or dripping chemicals with aluminum foil. Chemicals used for removing stains can damage the finish of a table or countertop and then transfer a new stain to the rug.

*Sponging:* When directions call for sponging, use this procedure. Moisten a piece of absorbent material with the appropriate stain remover. Sponge the stain from the edges towards the center. Use a pulling and pinching action on the pile to wipe off the stain. Avoid moistening areas outside of the stain with the stain remover. As soon as the absorbent material picks up stain, discard it and use new absorbent material. Your goal is to pick up and remove stain and not merely move the stain around. Check the back of the rug and remove any stain there, as well.

Figure 9-1. This diagram shows how staining materials should be wiped up from a rug. The direction of wiping is towards the center of the stain to minimize the spread of staining materials.

126

*Solidified staining materials:* For solid staining materials that have dried, break up the solid and remove as much as you can before using any liquid solvent. Use a dull-bladed kitchen knife and a stiff brush. Vacuum remaining particles from the rug. These solid staining materials include mud, clay, tar, chewing gum and food. By removing as much solid staining material as possible, you will minimize stain transfer by the seepage of the solvent.

Place an absorbent pad under the stain and a pad dampened with the recommended stain remover on top of the stain. Allow the stained area to soak until the hardened material has softened. This may take half an hour to several hours. Keep the stain damp by adding more stain remover as needed.

*Flushing:* Flushing the stain is necessary to remove released staining material and to remove stain removal chemicals. When the directions call for flushing, place clean absorbent material under the stain, then add the proper stain remover in small amounts with a medicine dropper or a container from which you can pour slowly. Do not add stain remover faster than the absorbent material can soak it up. Keep the treated area as small as possible. Change the absorbent material several times as you flush the stain. Flushing is one of the most important steps in stain removal. If a stain removal chemical remains in the rug, it may later damage the rug or cause another stain.

**Specific stain removal procedures**

Most stains are classified into eight groups. Stains which do not fall into these groups are listed alphabetically. It may not be necessary to go through all the steps described to remove the stain. When all the stain is gone, or when you have finished all the steps, wash the rug. In removing stains, work carefully and patiently. Often, the result depends as much on the way the job is done as on the remover used.

## GROUP 1 STAINS

| | | |
|---|---|---|
| Adhesive tape | Furniture wax | Ointment or salve |
| Automobile wax | Grease | Paint |
| Calamine lotion | Hair spray | Putty |
| Crayon, wax or grease | Hand lotion | Rouge |
| Eyebrow pencil | India ink | Shoe dye, black |
| Eye liner | Insecticides | Shoe polish, except white |
| Eye shadow | Lard | Smoke |
| Face powder | Lubricating Oil | Soot |
| Felt-tip marker ink | Facial makeup | Tar |
| Floor wax | Mascara | Typewriter ribbon ink |
| Furniture polish | Nose drops | |

1. Sponge with drycleaning solvent.
2. Sponge with dry spotter. Keep stain moist with dry spotter and blot occasionally with absorbent material. Continue as long as stain is being removed.
3. Flush with drycleaning solvent.
4. Repeat steps 2 and 3 until no more stain is removed.
5. Allow to dry completely.
6. Sponge with water.
7. Apply wet spotter and a few drops of ammonia and sponge. Keep stain moist with wet spotter and ammonia and blot occasionally with absorbent material. Continue as long as stain is being removed.
8. Flush with water.
9. Repeat steps 7 and 8 until no more stain is removed.

## GROUP 2 STAINS

| | | |
|---|---|---|
| Cake frosting | Cocoa | Milk |
| Catsup | Cream | Pudding |
| Cheese | Egg yolk | Salad dressing |
| Cheese sauce | Gravy | Sauces |
| Chili sauce | Ice cream | Soups containing vegetables |
| Chocolate | Mayonnaise | Steak sauce |

1. Sponge with dry cleaning solvent.

2. Sponge with dry spotter. Keep stain moist with dry spotter and blot occasionally with absorbent material. Continue as long as any stain is being removed.

3. Flush with drycleaning solvent.

4. Repeat steps 2 and 3 until no more stain is removed.

5. Allow to dry completely.

6. Sponge with water.

7. Apply a few drops of detergent and a few drops of ammonia and sponge. Keep stain moist with detergent and ammonia and blot occasionally with absorbent material.

8. Flush with water. It is important to remove all ammonia.

9. Soak in a solution of 1 quart warm water and 1 tablespoon enzyme product for 30 minutes. Rinse with water.

10. For chocolate stains, bleach with hydrogen peroxide. Wet the stain with hydrogen peroxide and add a drop or two of ammonia. Add more hydrogen peroxide and a drop of ammonia as needed to keep stain moist. Do not bleach longer than 15 minutes. Rinse thoroughly with water.

## GROUP 3 STAINS

| | | |
|---|---|---|
| Aftershave lotion | Eye drops | Mucus |
| Bath oil | Fish glue | Sherbet |
| Blood (dried) | Fish slime | Starch |
| Body discharge | Hide glue | Vomit |
| Egg white | Mouthwash | |

1. Soak area in a solution of 1 quart warm water, ½ teaspoon detergent, and 1 tablespoon ammonia for 15 minutes.

2. Sponge and blot occasionally with absorbent material. Continue as long as any stain is being removed.

3. Soak another 15 minutes in the solution used in step 1.

4. Rinse with water. It is important to remove all ammonia.

5. Soak in a solution of 1 quart warm water and 1 tablespoon enzyme product for 30 minutes.

6. Wash area.

7. For all stains except blood, repeat step 5, then wash again.

8. For a blood stain that is not completely removed, wet the stain with hydrogen peroxide and add a drop of ammonia. Do not bleach longer than 15 minutes. Rinse with water.

## GROUP 4 STAINS

Airplane glue
Carbon paper
Carbon typewriter ribbon
Contact cement
Corn remover
Cuticle oil

Cuticle remover
Fingernail hardener
Household cement
Lacquer
Fingernail polish
Mimeograph ink

Mimeograph correction fluid
Mucilage
Plastic
Plastic glue
Solder, liquid
Varnish

1. Sponge with drycleaning solution.
2. Sponge with dry spotter. Keep stain moist with dry spotter and blot occasionally with absorbent material. Continue as long as any stain is being removed.
3. Flush with drycleaning solvent.
4. Repeat steps 2 and 3 until no more stain is removed. Allow to dry.
5. Apply amyl acetate to stain and cover with a pad of absorbent material dampened with amyl acetate. Keep moist for 15 minutes, blotting occasionally with absorbent material. Sponge. When not working on the stain, keep it covered with an inverted bowl to minimze evaporation.
6. Flush with drycleaning solvent.

## GROUP 5 STAINS

Beer
Caramelized sugar
Casein glue
Coffee
Cordials
Corn syrup
Cough syrup
Fruit
Fruit juices

Fruit preserves
Home permanent
Jam and jelly
Maple syrup
Mixed drinks
Molasses
Mud
Shaving cream

Soft drinks
Suntan lotion
Tea
Toothpaste
Vegetables
Vinegar, colored
Whiskey
Wine

1. Soak in a solution of 1 quart warm water, ½ teaspoon detergent, and 1 tablespoon vinegar for 15 minutes.
2. Rinse with water.
3. Sponge with alcohol.
4. Wash.
5. Soak in a solution of 1 quart warm water and 1 tablespoon enzyme product for 30 minutes.
6. Wash.

## GROUP 6 STAINS

Antiperspirant
Candy (except chocolate)
Deodorant
Fabric dye, red
Food coloring, red

Hair dye, red
Ink, red
Mercurochrome
Merthiolate
Metaphen

Perspiration
Picric acid
Stamp pad ink, red
Urine
Watercolor paint, red

1. Soak in a solution of 1 quart warm water, ½ teaspoon detergent, and 1 tablespoon ammonia for 30 minutes.
2. Rinse with water.
3. Soak in a solution of 1 quart warm water and 1 tablespoon vinegar for 1 hour.
4. Rinse with water. Dry.
5. Apply alcohol and sponge. Keep stain moist with alcohol and blot occasionally with clean absorbent material. Continue as long as any stain is being removed.
6. Remove with water.

## GROUP 7 STAINS

Bluing
Fabric dye, all colors except red and yellow
Food coloring, all colors except red and yellow
Gentian violet
Hair dye, black or brown

Ink, black, blue, green or violet
Shoe dye, brown
Stamp pad ink, all colors except red and yellow
Watercolor paint, all colors except red and yellow

1. Soak in a solution of 1 quart warm water, ½ teaspoon detergent, and 1 tablespoon vinegar for 30 minutes. Agitate occasionally.
2. Rinse with water. Dry.
3. Apply alcohol to stain and cover with a pad of absorbent material dampened with alcohol. Let stand as long as any stain is being removed. Change pad as it picks up stain. Press pad hard onto the stain each time you check it. Keep stain and pad moist with alcohol.
4. Flush with alcohol. Allow to dry.
5. Soak in a solution of 1 quart warm water, ½ teaspoon detergent and 1 tablespoon ammonia for 30 minutes.
6. Rinse with water.

| | | |
|---|---|---|
| Asphalt | Cod liver oil | Peanut oil |
| Butter | Corn oil | Rubber cement |
| Castor Oil | Linseed oil | Safflower oil |
| Chewing gum | Olive oil | Vegetable oil |
| Coconut oil | | |

1. Place clean absorbent material under the stain. Apply drycleaner solvent and cover stain with a pad of absorbent material dampened with drycleaning solvent. Change the absorbent material as it pick up stain. Keep stain and pad moist with solvent.

2. Apply dry spotter. Cover stain with a pad dampened with dry spotter. Remove pad every five minutes and sponge. Continue the alternate soaking and sponging until all stain has been removed.

3. Flush with dry cleaning solvent. Allow to dry.

## Miscellaneous Stains

### Acids

1. Sponge with water and ammonia.
2. Flush with water.
3. Add more ammonia and flush with water again.
   Note: Strong acids will cause permanent damage.

### Alkalies

1. Sponge with water and vinegar.
2. Flush with water.
3. Add more vinegar and flush with water again.
   Note: Strong alkalies will cause permanent damage.

### Black walnut

1. Sponge with water.
2. Apply wet spotter and a few drops of vinegar, then sponge. Keep stain moist with wet spotter and vinegar. Blot occasionally with clean absorbent material. Continue as long as any stain is being removed.

### Ballpoint pen ink

1. Apply lukewarm glycerine. Sponge. Blot frequently by pressing hard on the stain with absorbent material. It is important to remove loosened stain immediately. Keep stain moist with glycerine. Continue as long as any stain is being removed.
2. Flush with water.
3. Apply wet spotter. Sponge.
4. Add several drops of ammonia and continue to sponge.
5. Flush with water.
6. Repeat steps 3 through 5 until no more stain is removed.
7. Flush with water.

### Candle wax

1. Scrape with spoon edge to remove wax.
2. Sponge with drycleaning solvent until all wax has been removed.
3. If any stain is left, apply wet spotter and a few drops of ammonia. Sponge.
4. Flush with water.
5. Repeat steps 3 and 4 until no more stain is removed.

## Grass

1. Sponge with drycleaning solvent as long as any stain is being removed.
2. Allow to dry.
3. Apply amyl acetate and rub stain with a pad of absorbent material dampened with amyl acetate.
4. Flush with drycleaning solvent and allow to dry.
5. Sponge with water.
6. Add a small amount of wet spotter and several drops of vinegar. Sponge.
7. Flush with water and allow to dry.
8. Sponge with alcohol and rub with pad dampened with alcohol.

## Lipstick

1. Apply drycleaning solvent and dry spotter and blot immediately with absorbent material.
2. Repeat step 1 until no more stain is removed. If stain begins to spread, flush immediately with drycleaning solvent. Then continue to repeat step 1.
3. Let all drycleaning solvent evaporate.
4. Sponge with water.
5. Apply wet spotter and a few drops of ammonia. Blot frequently with absorbent material.
6. Flush with water.
7. Apply wet spotter and a few drops of vinegar. Sponge frequently with absorbent material.
8. Flush with water. Allow to dry.
9. Sponge with alcohol, allow to dry.

## Mildew

1. Brush off powdered residue.
2. Flush with drycleaning solvent.
3. Apply dry spotter and amyl acetate. Sponge with dry spotter.
4. Flush with drycleaning solvent and allow to dry.
5. Sponge with water.
6. Apply wet spotter and vinegar. Sponge.

7. Flush with water and allow to dry.
8. Apply alcohol and pat stain with pad dampened with alcohol.
9. Flush with alcohol.
10. Repeat steps 8 and 9 until no more stain is removed.
11. Allow to dry.

## Mustard

1. Remove excess mustard.
2. Flush with drycleaning solvent and sponge.
3. Allow to dry.
4. Sponge with water.
5. Apply wet spotter and vinegar and sponge.
6. Flush with water.
7. Repeat steps 5 and 6 until no more stain is removed.
8. If any stain is left, wet the stain with hydrogen peroxide and add a drop of ammonia. Do not bleach longer than 15 minutes.
9. Flush with water.

## Shellac

1. Sponge with drycleaning solvent.
2. Apply dry spotter and sponge.
3. Flush with drycleaning solvent.
4. Apply alcohol and sponge.
5. Flush with alcohol.

## White shoe polish

1. Sponge with drycleaning solvent.
2. Apply dry spotter and sponge.
3. Flush with drycleaning solvent.
4. Repeat steps 1 to 3 until no more stain is removed.
5. Sponge with amyl acetate.
6. Flush with drycleaning solvent and allow to dry.
7. Sponge with water.
8. Add a few drops of vinegar and sponge.
9. Flush with water.
10. Repeat steps 7 to 9 until no more stain is removed.

*Unknown stains*

1. Sponge with drycleaning solvent.
2. Apply dry spotter and sponge.
3. Flush with drycleaning solvent.
4. Repeat steps 1 to 3 until no more stain is removed.
5. Apply amyl acetate and sponge.
6. Flush with drycleaning solvent and allow to dry.
7. Sponge with water. Add wet spotter and a few drops of vinegar. Sponge.
8. Apply wet spotter and a few drops of ammonia and sponge.
9. Allow to dry.
10. Sponge with alcohol and pat with a pad of absorbent material dampened with alcohol.
11. Allow to dry.

1. M. Boyle, *Textile Dyes, Finishes and Auxilliaries,* Garland Publishing, Inc., 1977

# Chapter 10

# Use, Care, Storage and Display

Oriental rugs, like other textiles, are fragile compared to many domestic objects. Eventually, oriental rugs are destroyed by reasonable use. They are not "over-engineered" in the manner of a cast iron stove that could last an eternity of reasonable use. However, if rugs are viewed more as art works than floor coverings, then special measures for their preservation are justified.

Many of the measures for the use, care, storage and display of oriental rugs in this chapter are merely common sense. But, sometimes reminders of common sense are helpful. Some of the measures are more appropriate for rugs as art objects. The measures you actually use are the true indicators of your valuation of a rug—a valuation somewhere between household expendable and work of art.

## Using Oriental rugs

Consider the condition, type and value of a rug in deciding where to place it. A fragile rug or killim will not last long in high-traffic areas such as halls and entryways. Rugs in high-traffic areas should be in full pile. The resiliance of pile protects the knots. But, knots without pile are not so effective in protecting the foundation. The rate of wear down to the foundation speeds up rapidly once the knots are exposed.

A recent decorating fad is to place small oriental rugs in the kitchen. This is the wrong location for a rug of any value. Food stains and heavy use will destroy such a rug fairly quickly.

Among Near-Eastern villagers and nomads, it is customary to remove shoes or boots when entering houses or tents. Most older nomadic, tribal and village rugs are not intended to be walked on with shoes and boots. They are not designed to withstand the constant friction of leather or the torturous pressures of spike or high heels. Accordingly, they should not be used for high-traffic areas. Contemporary factory-made oriental rugs are a different matter. They are constructed to hold up under normal Western usage.

Oriental rugs in use are protected from hard friction and crushing wear by placing them on pads or other carpets. The resiliency of underlying materials allows the rugs to flex and this promotes much longer wear. As an added benefit, the rug is more comfortable to walk on. Fiber pads are preferable to foam rubber. Foam rubber tends to harden and then crumble. Resiliency is lost and the rubber particles work their way into the back of the rug.

Cut rug pads so they are one inch smaller than the rug, all the way around the edge. Then, the rug edge will conceal the padding. Fiber pads have a tendency to flatten and spread slightly at the edges. The one-inch allowance provides clearance for this spreading.

Before cutting a pad, measure the rug carefully and check the corners with a large square. You may find the rug is a quadrilateral other than a rectangle. To cut fiber pads, use a heavy-duty Xacto knife. Mark the cut line on the pad with a felt tip pen. Then, use a metal straight edge to guide the knife. Considerable pressure or multiple strokes are needed. A wooden board can be placed under the cut line and pad to protect under surfaces. Pads can be pieced together using two or three-inch gaffers tape. This is a wide adhesive fabric tape sold in hardware stores or major photo supply stores.

Wear will be more evenly distributed if rugs in high-traffic areas are reversed each year. This end-to-end reversal is very desirable even though you don't notice annual wear. Once the knots are exposed in a particular area of the rug, wear will proceed much more rapidly. Reversing the rug will preserve the pile and delay wear exposure of the knots.

Use coasters to protect rugs where furniture rests on the rug. Shift furniture locations or reverse rugs annually so that crushed pile can "relax."

## Caring for rugs

It's a good idea to vacuum rugs in use often. Vacuuming prolongs the period between washes and reduces rug wear. Rugs in high-traffic areas should be vacuumed once a week. Use a brushless vacuum nozzle for greatest efficiency. If your vacuum cleaner has a power-driven rotating brush at the nozzle, never pass the nozzle over rug ends. Rotating brushes loosen fringes, end wefts and end knots.

How often should a rug be washed? Frequent washing can weaken a rug. This is offset by the fact that rug fibers are cut by entrapped soil particles. There's no rule-of-thumb as to the frequency of washing. Consider these questions in deciding whether a rug needs a wash:

- Does soil come off on your hand when you rub the pile, even after vacuuming?
- Aside from abrash, are there differences in the shade of similar light colored areas?
- Has the rug been exposed to heavy traffic?
- Does the rug have a stale or dusty smell?

A positive answer to any two of these questions suggests the rug needs a wash.

Of course, you know that a rug with foundation damage should not be used. Where warps or wefts are broken in the foundation, the selvage or ends, the damage will spread rapidly under the stress of use. Either repair the damage promptly or take the rug out of service.

Clean up spills right away. Scrape up solid materials and blot up liquids. Blot from the edges of the spill towards the center of the spill. After all free liquid is blotted up, surface clean the spill area. If the spilled substance may stain, use the appropriate stain removal techniques.

Finally, it's a good idea to carefully inspect rugs at least once each year. Look for wear or damage that should be repaired before the problem grows.

## Storing rugs

The area where rugs are stored should not be subject to wide temperature variation. Some humidity is alright, but humidity should not be high enough to support mildew. Optimum storage conditions are 50% relative humidity and a temperature of 70°F. Don't place rugs in storage unless they are clean. Soiled rugs invite insect attack and mildew.

Periodically, inspect stored rugs. The only way you can be absolutely sure the rugs are not being attacked by insects is to check them. Moth repellant products are not entirely dependable. Though their use is recommended, do not rely on them to the exclusion of regular inspections.

Roll rugs up for storage. It's best to store rolled rugs horizontally rather than on end. Rugs will be damaged along crease lines if they are folded for long-term storage.

Regular brown wrapping paper can be used to protect most rugs in storage. Never store rugs in plastic bags or plastic wrapping. The rugs should be able to absorb moisture from the atmosphere and release moisture into the atmosphere. For very valuable rugs, acid-free tissue paper is placed on the rug and rolled up with the rug. Heavy acid-free paper is then used to wrap the rolled rug. Acid-free paper and other conservation materials are supplied by:

The Hollinger Corporation
Post Office Box 6185
3810 South Four Mile Run Drive
Arlington, VA 22206

Process Materials Corporation
301 Veterans Boulevard
Rutherford, NJ 07070

## Displaying rugs on walls

Increasingly, fine rugs and collectors' rugs are displayed on walls. The motive is greater visibility and protection for the rug. But, a rug displayed on the wall is exposed to a whole new set of hazards. These hazards can be eliminated or reduced depending on the location and manner of display.

Let's consider the risks posed by the location of the rug. These include:

- Fading. Consistent exposure to direct sunlight will fade a rug. Do not locate rugs so they are regularly exposed to direct sunlight. If there is no alternative location, rugs can be protected with ultra violet filtering plexiglass (UF-3). Contact a local museum to find the nearest supplier of conservation materials.
- Dust condensation. If rugs are hung against a relatively cool surface in a room, fine dust in the air will be deposited on the rug. Avoid mounting rugs in such locations.
- Dessication. Do not hang rugs above radiators or hot air registers. The long-term effect is to dry out and embrittle the fibers.

Materials used in connection with display can cause damage. Metal in combination with moisture and air pollutants will corrode fibers where there is contact. Accordingly, nails, screws, hooks, staples, suspension rings and wire should not be used in mounting in such a way that they actually touch the rug. Direct contact with raw wood can produce staining and corrosion.

Figure 10-1. This shows how rugs should *not* be mounted. A finely woven, Hereke, silk prayer rug was glued to a fiberglass backing. Adhesives should never be used in mounting fabrics.

So, wood surfaces must be covered with some other fabric (preferably unbleached, unstarched muslin) where contact with the rug is possible.

Wall display, if incorrectly done, can structurally damage a rug. The weight of the rug can permanently stretch warps and wefts, producing scalloping at the suspension points, bellying and wrinkles. To avoid structural damage, the mounting system must provide even support for the rug. We'll describe three such mounting systems: permanent frame mounting, suspension rings and Velcro mounting.

## Frame mounting

For permanent frame mounting, a frame the same size as the rug is constructed. This mounting system is used only for small rectangular rugs, six feet by six feet or less. Frames can be built for other quadralaterals, but this becomes quite complicated. The frame is covered with muslin and the rug is stitched to the muslin. Here are the steps for permanent frame mounting:

1. Measure the rug carefully and check that the corners are square. Careful measurement is important since the frame is built to the exact size of the rug.

2. Stock to build the frame is sanded pine, two inches by three-quarter inch and free of knots.

3. Carefully measure and cut the pieces of wood to size. All pieces are joined using one and one-half inch countersunk wood screws. The thickness of the frame, front-to-back, is two inches.

4. Internal bracing consists of two cross pieces. These are inserted so that front-to-back thickness of both pieces is one and one-half inch.

5. For large frames, mitered diagonal internal corner braces are used in addition to cross braces.

6. Cut a piece of unbleached, starch-free muslin three and one-half inches larger than the frame at all edges. It may be necessary to sew two or more pieces of muslin together for larger frames.

7. The muslin is stretched tightly over the frame and stapled to the back. There is sufficient fabric so that the cut edge is folded under when it is stapled.

8. First, staple the center of opposite sides, pulling the muslin taut as you do so. Then, continue stapling around the edges using a one-half inch staple spacing. Adjust the tightness of the muslin as stapling proceeds to remove tension wrinkles.

9. Screw eyes and heavy wire can be installed on the inside of the frame for support in hanging.

10. Use cotton thread matching selvage and end colors. Stitch the rug to the muslin at the edges of the frame with whip stitches at a quarter-inch spacing.

11. Rugs should be tacked to the Muslin with stitches in the open areas from the back of the frame. A curved upholstery needle can be used for this purpose. Tack the rugs with a row of stitches across the open areas at a vertical spacing of about two feet.

ing, rings are attached to an unbleached, unstarched muslin strip. The strip is sewn to the back of the rug close to the edge that will be uppermost. Here are the steps:

1. You will need unbleached, unstarched muslin and plastic or metal rings about one inch in diameter.

2. Cut the muslin into a strip so it can be hemmed on both edges to a finished width of one and one-half inches. The length of the strip is a little less than the width of the rug.

3. After hemming the strip, sew the rings to the strip at three-inch intervals. Each ring is attached at three points, the bottom and each side.

4. The strip with rings is sewn to the rug with cotton thread using a whip stitch on each side of the strip.

5. The strip is sewn across the top end of the rug.

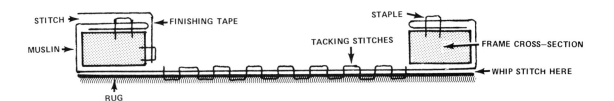

Figure 10-2. A cross-section of a rug mounted on a frame. On the right is a section of the frame with muslin folded and stapled in place for simple mounting. On the left, a strip of finishing tape is sewn and stapled in place to give the back of the frame a more finished appearance.

## Suspension rings

Suspension rings can be used to hang rugs. But, since suspension rings can be used conveniently along one edge only, they should not be used to hang a rug larger than four feet by four feet. For this system of mount-

6. Cut a wooden batten the width of the rug and drive large upholstery tacks into the batten at three-inch intervals to match the ring spacing. The rings will hang on these tacks.

7. Attach the wooden batten to the wall and hang the rug from it.

## Velcro mounting

Velcro can be purchased by the yard. It consists of two tapes. One tape is the hook side and the other is the loop side. The loop side has a fuzzy texture. To mount a rug for wall display using Velcro, follow these steps:

1. Prepare strips of unbleached muslin that are hemmed on both edges and that are one-half inch wider than the Velcro tape.

2. Sew the loop or fuzzy tape to the center of the hemmed muslin strip, leaving one-quarter inch at either edge.

3. Using a whip stitch, sew both edges of the muslin strip along the top end of the rug. A strip of loop Velcro is sewed across the width of the rug at two-foot vertical intervals.

4. With a staple gun, staple the hooked Velcro tape to wooden battens or strips. Staple spacing is one-half inch along both edges of the tape. The wood strips are as long as the rug is wide.

5. Nail or screw the wood strips to the wall at the same vertical spacing as the loop tapes of Velcro sewed to the rug. Measurement of spacing must be exact to assure that the loop tapes on the rug mesh with the hook tapes on the wall. The rug can be temporarily hung from the top strip to mark the location of the Velcro tapes on the wall.

6. Because of the width of the Velcro tapes, there can be some slight vertical adjustments when the rug is pressed against the wall for mounting.

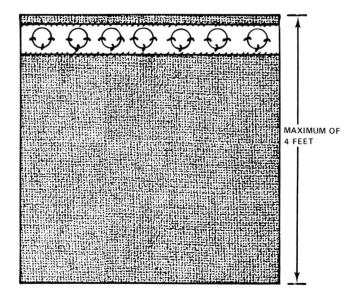

MAXIMUM OF 4 FEET

Figure 10-3. Here, suspension rings are sewn to a hemmed muslin strip. The strip is then whip-stitched to the back of the rug.

140

# Glossary

This glossary defines structural weaving and repair terms, generic terms relating to structure and function applied to pile fabrics and Near-eastern flatweaves, dye terms and a few terms describing design motifs. It does not present terms used in classifying rugs by source or origin. Where a foreign term is used, the derivation is indicated by the letter in brackets: (P) for Persian, (A) for Arabic, and (T) for Turkish or Turkmen.

## A

**abrash** (P)     A change in color in the field and border due to differences in wool or dye batches. The color change extends across the rug, weft-wise. Abrash is more likely to occur at the top of a rug, as beginning yarn batches are used up, than at the bottom of a rug.

**abrisham** (P)     Silk.

**aniline dyes**     Aniline dyes are synthetic dyes. They were the first manufactured chemical dyes and were introduced in the Near East about 1870. Aniline dyes fade and change color with exposure to light.

**alpaca**     A domesticated South American animal related to the llama. It has long silky wool used in South American weaving.

**Arabic numbers, dates**     Dates are sometimes woven into rugs using Arabic calligraphy. These numbers translate as follows:

$$1 = \boldsymbol{I} \quad 2 = \boldsymbol{N} \quad 3 = \boldsymbol{\mu} \quad 4 = \boldsymbol{\varepsilon}, \boldsymbol{\mu} \quad 5 = \boldsymbol{O}, \boldsymbol{O}$$
$$6 = \boldsymbol{\gamma}, \boldsymbol{\gamma} \quad 7 = \boldsymbol{V} \quad 8 = \boldsymbol{\Lambda} \quad 9 = \boldsymbol{q} \quad 0 = \boldsymbol{+}, \boldsymbol{\bullet}$$

The Arabic date is converted into a European date using this equation:

$$\text{Arabic Date} + 622 - \frac{\text{Arabic Date}}{33.7} = \text{European Date}$$

**ara-khachi** (T)     Middle or main stripe in a rug border.

**asmylak** (T)     A five sided Turkmen camel trapping.

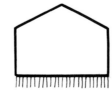

| | |
|---|---|
| **asymmetric knot** | The Persian (Farsibaff) or Senneh knot. This knot may be open to the right or to the left. |

|  | |
|---|---|
| Open to the left | Open to the right |

| | |
|---|---|
| **audience rug, triclinium** | In certain Islamic countries it was customary in important dwellings to arrange rugs in the main chamber as shown. |

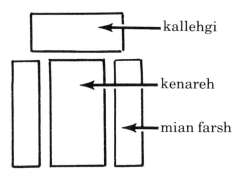

kallehgi

kenareh

mian farsh

When a single rug is woven to represent this arrangement, it is known as an audience rug or triclinium rug (after the three couches surrounding the eating table in ancient Rome). These terms are not native to Islamic countries nor do they correctly suggest the function of the rug in a household.

| | |
|---|---|
| **azo dyes** | Synthetic dyes introduced about 1880 including Ponceau 2R, Amaranth and Roccelline. Many of these dyes have a tendency to run. |

**B**

| | |
|---|---|
| **baff** (P) | Knot in Persian. |
| **bala-khachi** (T) | Narrow borders on either side of a main border. |
| **band-e Kenareh** (P) | Heavy selvage warps in a pile rug. |

| | |
|---|---|
| **bast** | Woody fibers used for weaving such as flax, hemp, or jute. |
| **beshek** (T) | Bedding bag. |
| **bloom** | To add ingredients to the dye bath which increase the brightness of colors. |
| **border** | A design around the edge of a rug and enclosing the field. The border usually includes a wide band of repeating design called the main border. |
| **bokche** (T) | A Turkmen envelope-like bag consisting of a square flat-weave with pile woven triangles at each side of the rectangle. The triangular pieces are folded inwards to form a container. |
| **boteh** | A pear-shaped figure often used in oriental rug designs. It has been thought to represent a leaf, a bush or a pinecone. The boteh figure is characteristic of the Paisley pattern. |

## C

| | |
|---|---|
| **cable weft** | When warps are offset or depressed, wefts are alternately straight or bending in their passage through the warps. The straight and tight weft is termed a "cable" weft and the bending weft is termed a "sinuous" weft. |

| | |
|---|---|
| **carding** | To comb fibers prior to spinning with brushes having wire bristles. Woolens are wool yarns that are carded. |
| **cartoon** | A grid on paper with spaces colored to guide rug weavers in selecting pile yarns to execute a rug design. |
| **cartouche** | An enclosed area in the field or border containing an inscription, name or date. |
| **chain stitch** | A crochet stitch consisting of successive loops used to lock the final weft in place at the end of a rug. |

**chintamani**

Ottoman court motif of three balls above two cloudbands. Also referred to as the badge of Tamarlane.

**chrome dyes**

A group of modern synthetic dyes that are used with a mordant of potassium bichromate. These dyes are fast and non-fugitive.

**cicim** (T)

An Anatolian flatweave curtain or blanket composed of woven bands sewn together. Pronounced "jijim." See "jij-im."

**cloud band**

A curving, horseshoe-shaped motif originating in China.

**cochineal**

A red dye derived from the dried female bodies of the scale insect, Dactylopius coccus.

**corrosion**

See "etching."

**crewel yarn**

A thin, lightweight, 2-ply, medium-twist yarn.

**crocking**

A loss of dye color at points of friction or wear.

**D**

**dashgah** (T)

Loom.

**dhurrie, durrie**

A flatwoven carpet of India, frequently made of cotton.

**divari** (P)

Vertical carpet loom.

**dozar** (P)

A rug size—about 6 ft. by 4 ft. The term is not correctly applied to a rug designed as a sleeping mat. "Dozar" means two zars.

## E

**elem** (T), **skirt**　　　End panel of Turkmen bag faces and rugs outside of the main border.

**ensi, engsi** (T)
**pardeh** (P)　　　A felt or pile rug hung over the door of Turkmen tents. The pile ensi design usually includes four quadrants with these divisions creating a cross or hatchli in the center of the rug. See "katchli."

**esperek** (P), **zalil**　　　A yellow dye obtained from the flowers of the yellow lark-spur, Delphinium zalil.

**etching, corrosion**　　　The loss of pile in colored areas of a rug where a dye was used that contains corrosive salts, usually areas dyed black or brown.

## F

**false selvage**　　　See "selvage, false."

**family prayer rug**　　　See "saph."

**farsh** (P)　　　Floor covering.

**farsibaff**　　　Asymmetric or Persian pile knot.

**field**　　　The portion of a rug design enclosed by borders. The field may be unoccupied or contain medallions or an all-over pattern.

**figure eight stitch**　　　An overcasting stitch used for selvages containing two or more warps or warp bundles. The "8" is the path of the overcasting yarn as it passes around the warps.

**flatweave**　　　A fabric woven without knotted pile.

**float**　　　In a plain weave, carrying a weft over two or more adjacent warps or carrying a warp over two or more adjacent wefts.

**flosh** (T)　　　Mercerized cotton polished to look like silk. Sometimes referred to as "Turkish silk." Rugs made of mercerized cotton.

**foundation**　　　The combination of warps and wefts in the body of a rug.

**fringe**

Warps extending from the foundation at the ends of a rug. These warps are treated in various ways to prevent wefts and knots from unraveling.

**fugitive dye**

The failure of a dye to retain its hue and shade. This failure may involve a change in hue as well as fading.

**fuschine**

A magenta aniline dye discovered in about 1859. This dye fades when exposed to light.

## G

**gaba, gabeh**

Coarsely woven rugs from south-western Iran made of undyed wool.

**garden carpet**

A design originally thought to represent the layout of a Persian garden with flower beds and streams. The term now refers to any rug that includes rectangular compartments, each containing some floral or botanic motif.

**gauge rod**

A rod used in Tibetan pile weaving. Pile yarn is looped over the gauge rod and around the warps. When the loops over the gauge rod are cut, a pile of consistent height is produced.

**gereh** (P)

Knot.

**gereh zadan** (P)

To knot into fringes.

**Ghiordes knot**

See "symmetric knot."

**gillim**

See "killim."

**ground**

The interlaced combination of warp and weft that is structurally essential to the fabric. In pile rugs, the "ground" may be referred to as the "foundation."

**guard stripe**

Stripes or lesser borders on either side of the main border. See "border."

**gul, gol**

A medallion of octagonal or angular shape used in Turkmen designs. Often, the gul is repeated to form an all-over pattern in the field. Certain Turkmen tribes are associated with specific guls as emblems of the tribe.

ERSARI        ERSARI

SARIQ        SALOR

TEKKE        YOMUD

YOMUD

**H**

**hali** (T)              Carpet (Pronounced "ha-la").

**hatchli, hatchlu**      See "katchli."

**heybeh** (T)        Saddle bag.

147

| | |
|---|---|
| **Herati pattern** | A design, usually repeated, consisting of a flower centered in a diamond with curving lanceolate leaves located outside the diamond and parallel to each side. |

| | |
|---|---|
| **hue** | Color from the spectrum or combination of such colors. |
| **I** | |
| **ikat** | A process in which fabric designs are created by tie-dyeing warps and/or wefts before they are used on the looms. A fabric produced by this process. |
| **indigo** | A blue vegetable dye derived from a member of the pea family. A yellow juice from the plant oxidizes to blue upon exposure to air. Indigo was chemically synthesized in 1880. |
| **J** | |
| **jijim, djidjim** (T) | A flatweave of narrow strips sewn together. |
| **jolam** (T) | See "tent band." |
| **jollar** | See "kapunuk." |
| **joval, juval, tschoval, chuval** (T) | A large bag, approximately 3 ft. by 6 ft., one surface of which may be covered with pile, used to store clothing. Often, only the pile face has survived. |

| | |
|---|---|
| **jufti knot** | A symmetric or asymmetric knot tied over four warps instead of the usual two warps. |

| | |
|---|---|
| **jute** | A fiber from the stem of the plant, Corchorus capsularis. Jute has been used in the pile of rugs from India. |

**K**

| | |
|---|---|
| **kallehgi, kelley** (P) | A long, narrow carpet in which length is at least twice the width, 5 ft. by 10 ft. or 8 ft. by 24 ft., for example. |
| **kapunuk** (T) | A pile fabric decoration for the inside of Turkmen tent doors. |

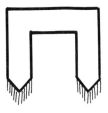

| | |
|---|---|
| **kardak** (P) | Carpet trimming knife. |
| **katchli, hatchlu, hatchli** (T) | The cross formed by the four panels in the design of an ensi. |
| **kejebe** (T) | A tent-like enclosure for the bride on the back of a camel in a Turkmen wedding procession. The kejebe is represented in Turkmen rugs by this shape: |

| | |
|---|---|
| **kelley** (P) | See "kalleghi." |
| **kenareh** (P) | Persian term for a runner, 2½ to 3½ ft. wide. |
| **kermes** (P) | A red dye prepared from a scale insect, Coccul ilicis, which infests oak trees. |
| **khorjin, kharjin** (P) | A saddle bag. |
| **killim** | A tapestry-woven rug. Also, the flatweave end of a rug. |
| **kork** (P) | Underhair of a goat or fine belly wool of a sheep. |
| **kufic** (A) | Used to describe border designs that are thought to be derived from an Arabic script. |

## L

| | |
|---|---|
| **lac** | A red dye made from a scale insect, Coccus laccae. |
| **lachak torang** (P) | Any design with corner and central medallions. |
| **lazy lines** | Diagonal lines visible from the back of the rug caused by successive rows of turnarounds of discontinuous wefts. This occurs when only a portion of the width of a rug is woven at one time. |

## M

| | |
|---|---|
| **macramé** (A) | Fringe. Used to describe off-loom weaving and knot work. From the Arabic for "knot." |
| **madder** | A red dye extracted from the root of the madder plant, Rubia tinctorium. Madder dye has been synthesized as the alzarine colors. "Alizari" is Arabic for madder. |
| **mafrash** (A) | A small bag, often with a pile face. A traveling or bedding bag. |
| **main border** | See "border." |
| **mako** (P) | Weaver's shuttle. |
| **Manchester** | See "merino." |

| | |
|---|---|
| **matn** (P) | Ground or field of a rug. |
| **mazarlik** (T) | A Turkish carpet with representations of trees and houses. Some believe such carpets are used to enfold the dead when carried to a cemetery. |
| **meander** | Any of a wide variety of continuous border designs that do not fill the band they occupy but alternate from side to side. |
| **medallion** | A large enclosed portion of a design usually located in the center of a field. Common shapes are diamonds, octagons and hexagons. |
| **"Memling" gul** | A motif named after Hans Memlinc, a 15th century artist whose works show rugs designed with the motif. |

| | |
|---|---|
| **mercerized** | Cotton thread whose strength and gloss has been increased by treating with alkali under pressure. |
| **merino** | A breed of sheep producing very fine wool. The merino was first raised in Spain. Australian merino wool is used in some rugs from Iran and India. "Manchester" is merino wool processed in Manchester, England. |
| **mian farsh** (P) | The middle carpet in the traditional Persian rug arrangement. See "audience rug." |
| **mihrab** (P) | The prayer niche in a mosque represented by the arch in a prayer rug. |
| **millefleurs** | A design composed of many flower blossoms, often occupying the field of a prayer rug, found in rugs from Iran and India. |

**mina khani** (P)    An over-all pattern consisting of two or more flower blossoms connected by a diamond lattice.

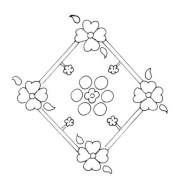

**mir-i-boteh** (P)    A design of multiple rows of botehs.

**mohair, mouher** (P)    Yarn or fabric made from the fleece of the Angora goat.

**mordant**    A product used in dyeing that reacts with the dye and fiber to fix the dye permanently to the fiber. Different mordants produce different hues and shades from the same dye.

**morghi** (P)    A hen. A design employing images of chickens.

**mori**    A term describing the weave of certain Pakistani and Indian rugs, specifically the absence of warp offset in these rugs.

**muska** (T)    A triangular design, supposed to have magical properties, derived from the shape of a pouch used to carry Koranic inscriptions or religious or shamanistic relics.

**N**

**namazlik** (T),
**naqsh doa** (P)    Prayer rug.

**naqsh** (P)    A design or pattern

**nassag-bafendeh** (P)    Weaver.

**node**    One loop of a pile knot around a warp when viewed from the back of a rug.

# O

**odjakhlik** (T)  A rug used in front of a fireplace.

**offset**  See "warp offset."

**ok-bash** (T)  Tent pole cover.

**overcasting**  A treatment of selvages consisting of a yarn wrapping or interweaving with yarn that is not continuous with foundation weft.

# P

**painting**  Applying dye, stain or color to the front of the rug after the rug is woven. Exposed foundation is sometimes painted to conceal wear.

**palas**  A Caucasian flatweave rug.

**pardeh**  See "ensi."

**pashm** (P)  Wool.

**Persian knot**  See "asymmetric knot."

**Persian yarn**  A soft-spun, 3-ply yarn made up of medium-twist 2-ply yarns.

**pile**  Nap of the rug. The tufts remaining after the knotted yarn is clipped.

**pillar rug**  A Chinese pile rug designed to be wrapped around a pillar or column. The design is not complete unless the edges of the rug abut.

**plain weave**  The simplest interlacing of warp and weft in which there is only one weft in each of two sheds composed of alternating warps.

**plug**  A piece from another rug sewn or woven into a hole in a rug.

**ply**  Two or more yarns spun together make a ply or plied yarn.

**prayer rug**  A rug with a representation of a mihrab or prayer niche. Columns may be shown supporting the arch and a lamp may be shown hanging from the apex of the arch. A double prayer rug is one showing a niche at either end as a mirror image. See "saph."

| | |
|---|---|
| **Prophet's green** | Shades of green derived from combinations of indigo blue and yellow obtained from either yellow larkspur or unripe berries of a plant of the buckthorn family. This was thought to be the color of Mohammed's banner. |
| **provenance** | The source or origin. When applied to rugs, provenance refers to the place of origin, the weavers of the rug and the time of origin. |
| **pu** (P) | A row of knots in a carpet. |
| **pud** (P) | Weft. |
| **pushti** | A Persian mat of about 3 ft. by 2 ft. |
| **Q** | |
| **qali** (P) | Any rug larger than about 6 ft. by 9 ft. |
| **R** | |
| **rang** (P) | Dye, color. |
| **rang-raz** (P) | Dyer. |
| **rang shodeh** (P) | "Color has been given." A painted rug. |
| **rofu** (P) | Repair. To repair so that it may not be evident. |
| **S** | |
| **"S" spun** | Yarn spun in a clockwise direction. The diagonal in the "S" suggests the direction of spin. |
| **sadden** | To add ingredients to the dye bath which mute or darken the color. |
| **saddle bags** | Two bags or pouches connected so they can be thrown over the back of a horse or donkey. The outside faces may be pile while the inside faces are flatwoven. Typically, a pair of bags is about 2 ft. by 4 ft. |
| **Safavid** | Refers to rugs made during the Safavid dynasty in Persia between 1500 and 1730. |
| **sajjada** (P) | Prayer rug. |

| | |
|---|---|
| **salt bag** | A bag of distinctive shape that may have a pile face. It is used to store salt or grain. |

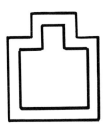

| | |
|---|---|
| **saph, saff** | A prayer rug containing multiple niches in a row, sometimes referred to as a family prayer rug. |
| **selvage, selvedge** | The edge warps of a rug and the foundation wefts passing around those warps. |
| **selvage, false** | Cords sewn or woven parallel to a rug edge to replace or reinforce original edge warps. |
| **Senneh knot** | See "asymmetric knot." |
| **sezar** (P) | Three zars. A rug approximately 7½ ft. by 5 ft. |
| **shade** | A hue with an admixture of white, black or grey. |
| **shed** | The opening formed through the warps when alternate warps are raised to permit the shuttle and weft to pass through the warps. There is one shed for each set of warps, depending on whether even or odd-numbered warps are raised. |
| **shoot, shot, pick** | A weft or the passage of a weft through a shed. |
| **shotori** (P) | Camel-colored or naturally brown sheep wool. |
| **sili** | See "zili." |
| **singles yarn** | An unplied yarn consisting of fibers all spun in the same direction. |
| **sinuous weft** | When warps are offset or depressed, wefts are alternately straight or bending in their passage through the warps. The bending weft is termed a "sinuous" weft and the straight weft is termed a "cable" weft. See "cable weft." |

| | |
|---|---|
| **sizing** | Starch or glue added to yarns or fabrics to increase their smoothness, stiffness or bulk. |
| **skein** | A coil of yarn. |
| **skirt** | See "elem." |
| **sofreh** (P) | A cloth on which food is served. |
| **soumak** | A flatwoven rug using supplementary wefts in a weft-wrapping technique, usually producing a herringbone effect. |
| **slit weave** | A tapestry weave in which wefts of different colors reverse direction on adjacent warps. Where several rows of wefts reverse direction on the same adjacent warps, a slit in the fabric results. |
| **Spainish knot** | A pile knot tied on a single warp. This knot is thought to have originated in North Africa. |

| | |
|---|---|
| **spandrel** | Designs spanning the corners of a rug and the areas in either corner above a mihrab. |
| **spin** | The relative direction of twist of yarns, "Z" spun or "S" spun. |
| **staple** | The average length of fibers in a yarn. |
| **supplementary weft** | A weft that is not structurally essential to a fabric that is added to create a textured or ornamental effect. |
| **supplementary weft float patterning** | Ornamentation of a ground fabric with supplementary wefts, continuous from selvage to selvage, that skip over two or more adjacent warps. |
| **suzanduz** (P) | Coarse needlework patterning on flatwoven rugs. The term is incorrectly applied to soumac weave. |
| **suzanni** (P) | Embroidered needlework used as wall hangings and bed covers. |

| | |
|---|---|
| **symmetric knot** | The Turkish (Turkbaff) or Giordes knot. This knot is tied on two warps as shown: |

## T

| | |
|---|---|
| **tamgas** | Nomadic livestock brand which may also be a tribal emblem woven into rugs. |
| **talim** (P) | A written description of the numbers of pile knots and their colors to create a specific design. Used in the production of factory rugs. |
| **tapestry weave** | Any one of a variety of weaves in which there are no supplementary wefts and the pattern or design is created by ground wefts that are not continuous from selvage to selvage. |
| **tapestry yarn** | A 4-ply, hard-spun yarn. |
| **tar** (P) | Warp. |
| **tent band, girth, jolam, yup** | Tent bands, visible from the inside of Turkmen tents, serve both structural and decorative purposes. Some tent bands are ornamented with pile. Tent bands are between 8 in. and 22 in. wide and about 40 ft. long. |
| **torba** (T) | A shallow bag hung from the tent structure. A torba is smaller than a joval. Pile knotting may be used on only one face of a torba. |
| **triclinium** | See "audience rug." |
| **tun** (P) | Warp. |
| **turnarounds** | In reweaving foundation, new warp reverses direction when it passes from one column of knot nodes to the next column of knot nodes. New weft reverses direction when it passes under a knot. These reversals of direction are called "turnarounds." |
| **Turkbaff** | See "symmetric knot." |

| | |
|---|---|
| **Turkish knot** | See "symmetric knot." |
| **twill** | A basic diagonal weave in which warps consistently skip 2, 3, 4 or 5 wefts or wefts consistently skip 2, 3, 4 or 5 warps. |

## V

| | |
|---|---|
| **vagier reh** (P) | "That which is gotten from something else." A sample rug. |
| **vakif** (A) | The Islamic practice of giving land, rugs or other assets to the mosque. |
| **vase carpet** | Carpets with a field filled by flowers and tendrils or a lattice with a vase located at one or both ends. |
| **verneh** | Caucasian flatweave rug. |
| **vordelik** (T) | Wall hanging. Silk rugs are often used in this manner. |

## W

| | |
|---|---|
| **warp** | Warps are the initial structural components of loom-woven fabrics. Parallel warp yarns run the length of the loom. Wefts are woven through the warps and pile knots are tied to the warps. |
| **warp faced** | In a balanced plain weave, warps and wefts are equally visible. In a warp faced fabric, warps are more closely spaced than wefts and wefts are concealed. |
| **warp offset, warp depression** | A set of warps can be held in a plane by tight supporting wefts (cable wefts) while alternate warps are permitted to lie in another plane due to loose and bending wefts (sinuous wefts). Alternate warps are seen to be depressed from the back of the rug. Warps may be offset to the extent that one warp may lie on top of another. See "cable weft." |
| **washing** | Rugs may be washed in chemical solutions to soften (bleach) colors and to increase the lustre of fibers. |
| **weft** | Wefts are yarns woven through warps by means of a shuttle. Wefts are horizontal or crosswise yarns when the fabric is viewed on a loom. |
| **weft chaining** | A weft wrapping technique similar to crochet work in which weft loops are pulled through each other as they pass around warps. |

| | |
|---|---|
| **weft faced** | In a balanced plain weave, warps and wefts are equally visible. In a weft faced fabric, wefts are more closely spaced than warps and warps are concealed. Because of the warp spacing dictated by pile knotting, end killims are usually weft faced. |
| **weft float brocade** | The use of supplementary wefts, not continuous from selvage to selvage, to create a design by skipping over warps. The ground fabric is usually a plain weave in oriental rugs. |
| **weft twining** | A weft wrapping method in which two wefts pass across warps, twisting together after each warp or at regular intervals. |
| **weft wrapping** | Any system by which wefts loop around warps rather than only interlacing or passing over and under warps. Soumak and weft chaining are two forms of weft wrapping. |
| **weld** | The plant, Reseda luteola, the stalks, leaves and flowers of which yield a yellow dye. |
| **whip stitch** | A simple stitch used in overcasting and to lock the final weft in rug ends. |
| **woolen** | A wool yarn of mixed staple that has been carded. Fibers are neither as long or as parallel as worsted yarn. |
| **worsted** | A wool yarn of long staple with fibers that have been combed prior to spinning. Combing produces more parallel fibers than carding. |

**Y**

| | |
|---|---|
| **yak-gereh** (P) | Asymmetric knot. |
| **yastik** (T) | A small Anatolian pillow face about 1½ ft. by 3 ft. |
| **yatak** (T) | Anatolian shaggy-pile rugs made as sleeping mats. |

**Z**

| | |
|---|---|
| **"Z" spun** | Yarn spun in a counter-clockwise direction. The diagonal lines in the "Z" suggest the direction of spin. |
| **zalil** | See "esperek." |

| | |
|---|---|
| **zar** (P) | Persian linear measure of about 41 or 44 inches. Also, gold. |
| **zaronim** (P) | A persian rug of about 5 ft. by 3½ ft. Literally, one and one-half zars. |
| **zili, sili** | A Caucasian flatweave. |
| **zilu** (P) | Woven cotton rug. |

References used in preparing this glossary include:

V. Birrell, *The Textile Arts*, Harper and Brothers, 1959.

P. Collingwood, *The Techniques of Rug Weaving*, Watson-Guptill, 1978.

A. de Franchis and J.T. Wertime, *Lori and Bakhtiyar Flatweaves*, Tehran Rug Society, 1976.

J.S. Herbert, *Affordable Oriental Rugs*, MacMillan Publishing Co., 1980.

G. Izmidlian, *Oriental Rugs and Carpets Today*, Hippocrene Books, Inc., 1977.

A.N. Landreau and W.R. Pickering, *From the Bosporus to Samarkand Flat-Woven Rugs*, The Textile Museum, 1969.

H.E. Wulff, *The Traditional Crafts of Persia*, Massachusetts Institute of Technology, 1966.

## ART CREDITS

| | | |
|---|---|---|
| Page 9 | Weaver at work | *Trades and Professions,* |
| Page 166 | Rug on display | Hart Publishing Co., Inc. |
| | | |
| Page 147 | Turkmen guls | A. Dowlatshahi, *Persian Designs* |
| Page 148 | Herati pattern | *and Motifs,* Dover Publications, |
| Page 152 | Mina khani | Inc. |

All other line art is the work of the author.

## TYPOGRAPHY CREDITS

Typographic composition was done by Tele Typography. The manuscript was scanned on a Kurzweil scanner by Omnitext, Inc.

# Oriental Rug Repair

# Index

166